WITHDRAWN

An Introduction to Scenic Design

AN INTRODUCTION TO SCENIC DESIGN

A. S. Gillette

DIRECTOR OF THE UNIVERSITY THEATRE
STATE UNIVERSITY OF IOWA

HARPER & ROW, PUBLISHERS

New York, Evanston, and London

LEWIS - CLARK
NORMAL SCHOOL
LIBRARY

47936

AN INTRODUCTION TO SCENIC DESIGN

Copyright © 1967 by A. S. Gillette. Printed in the United States of America. All rights reserved. No part of this book may be used or reproduced in any manner whatsoever without written permission except in the case of brief quotations embodied in critical articles and reviews. For information address Harper & Row, Publishers, Incorporated, 49 East 33rd Street, New York, N.Y. 10016.

Library of Congress Catalog Card Number: 67-11649

PN
2091
S8
G49

LEWIS – CLARK
NORMAL SCHOOL
LIBRARY

CONTENTS

Preface / ix

1. Background Studies for Stage Design / 1

2. An Approach to Scenic Design / 6

3. The Designer's Procedure / 18

4. Requirements for a Well-Designed Stage Setting / 30

5. Mechanical Drawing / 44

6. Perspective / 59

7. The Water Color Sketch / 79

8. The Designer's Plans / 92

9. Paint Shop Equipment / 108

10. Scene Painting / 127

11. Toward an Understanding of Style in Design / 143

12. Styles in Scenic Design / 149

13. European Scenic Design / 179

Bibliography / 205

Index / 207

ILLUSTRATIONS

PLATE

1. Organization chart   11
2. Color wheel   38
3. Scale of brilliance   39
4. Neutralization chart   40
5. Architect's rule   49
6. Drafting symbols   51
7. Alphabet and numerals   53
8. Orthographic projection   55
9. Isometric drawing   57
10. Oblique drawing   58
11. Cabinet drawing   58
12. Perspective: Receding lines   60
13. Auditorium and stage: Vertical section   62
14. Auditorium and stage: Horizontal plan   63
15. Perspective: Problem I   64
16. Perspective: Problem II   66
17. Perspective: Problem III   67
18. Perspective: Problem IV   69
19. Perspective: Problem V   69
20. Perspective: Problem VI   71
21. Perspective: Problem VII   72
22. Perspective: Problem VIII   73
23. Perspective: Problem IX   75
24. Perspective Problem X, Ground plan, *Anna Christie*   76

PLATE

25. Completed perspective, *Anna Christie*   76
26. Front elevations, *Anna Christie*   77
27. *Anna Christie*, State University of Iowa production   77
28. Thumbnail sketches, *Chancellor's Party*   80
29. Water color sketch, *Chancellor's Party*   81
30. Water color paint brushes   85
31. Water color mixing palettes   86
32. Master plan of stage   93
33. Ground plan, *Chancellor's Party*   96–97
34. Drafting conventions for stage ground plans   98
35. Front elevations, *Chancellor's Party*   100–101
36. Detail drawings   102
37. Pen and ink sketch, *Mississippi*   103
38. Vertical sight-line drawing   104
39. Horizontal sight-line drawing   104
40. Exhibition model   106
41. Graphed elevation   110

PLATE

42. Paint frame and
    boomerang   112
43. Scene paint storage
    bins   114
44. Rolling paint palette   117
45. Paint shop equipment   118
46. Shading   131
47. Spattering   132
48. Mask spattering   133
49. Scrumbling   134
50. Stippling   135
51. Dry brushing   136
52. Rolling   137
53. Crosshatching   137
54. Puddling   138
55. Stenciling   139
56. Stencil on frame   139
57. Straight edging   141
58. Naturalism,
    Pygmalion   151
59. Realism, *Calvario* and
    Death of a Salesman   152
60. Pictorial realism,
    Caliban   155
61. Suggestive realism,
    La Traviata   156
62. Stylization,
    Mrs. McThing,
    The Country Wife,
    Dark of the Moon,
    Ondine,
    The Doctor in Spite
    of Himself   160–162

PLATE

63. Formalism, *Caprices of*
    Marianne and *Hamlet*   164
64. Drapery setting, *The*
    Doctor's Dilemma   166
65. Space stage, *Othello*   167
66. Arena stage,
    Trespassers   168
67. Unit setting, model of
    the Studio Theatre,
    State University of
    Iowa   169
68. Architectural stage,
    the Tyrone Guthrie
    Theatre, Minneapolis,
    and the Stratford
    Festival Theatre,
    Stratford, Ontario   172–173
69. Expressionism, *The*
    Dream Play   175
70. Constructivism, *The*
    Duchess of Malfi   177
71. *Othello*   181
72. *Tom Sawyer*   183–184
73. *My Crime*   187
74. *Intrigue and Love* 189–191
75. *Talent and Its*
    Admirers   193–194
76. *Umka*   195–196
77. *The School for*
    Taxpayers   199
78. *The Beginning of*
    Life   201–202
79. *Life on Wheels*   203–204

PREFACE

THIS TEXT is intended primarily as an introduction to the field of scenic design and as a supplement to the lectures offered in a course on that subject in the Department of Speech and Dramatic Art at the State University of Iowa. The work is so arranged that it should also prove helpful to those directors of little theatres and to those teachers who have not had any special training in this subject who find themselves confronted with the problem of designing and painting scenery for their own productions.

The very nature of art itself precludes the supposition that anyone without a natural aptitude for design should expect to create outstanding designs merely by following the suggestions and rules listed in any book. Successful designs for the stage are based on a sound and thorough knowledge of the theatre and on the principles of good design. This knowledge must in turn be coupled with constant practice and a willingness to learn. However, the subjects treated in this book are so planned and arranged that the student or the practical theatre worker should find little difficulty in understanding the designer's procedure and method of working; this understanding should help him avoid many of the mistakes that are often learned at the artistic and financial expense of a production.

Just how does one acknowledge the assistance he receives from others, either directly or indirectly, once he has embarked on a program of writing? Where does one begin and to whom should he give credit? Certainly I make no claim that all the information contained in this book is original with me. I know that some of it was gained through association with the directors and colleagues with whom I have worked over the years, some came from bright and imaginative students, while some of it undoubtedly came from texts I used in my student days and many books I have since read. To single out for explicit acknowledgment all these sources is clearly beyond my memory, but to all those unnamed contributors I willingly acknowledge my deep gratitude.

I am especially indebted to Donald Oenslager, professor of design at Yale, for first introducing me to the excitement and pleasure of working in stage design; I am indebted to the Rockefeller Foundation for a grant that enabled me to study European design, and to the Graduate College of the State University of Iowa for a grant of time that made possible the completion of this book. Most of all I am grateful to my wife Josephine without whose assistance and encouragement this book would not have been written.

A. S. GILLETTE

An Introduction to Scenic Design

BACKGROUND STUDIES FOR STAGE DESIGN

It was opening night of the first production in our summer stock company in the Berkshires. The entire technical staff, all five of us students at the time, stood backstage nervously peeking at the action on stage from any vantage point we could find. We had reason to be worried. The setting was a two-room apartment with a separating partition extending from the back wall toward the audience. This partition had defied our best efforts at bracing and we were hoping that the weight of the ceiling would hold it in place in spite of the active stage business. As we watched through both the first and second acts it seemed steady enough and we began to breathe easier. But in the third act, after a particularly violent door slam, the partition began to lean and was obviously on its way down. The actors, too, had been well aware of our problems in bracing the wall and they had kept a furtive and cautious eye on the monster from the time we first wrestled it into place for the dress rehearsals. Leo Carroll, a veteran actor long accustomed to the flimsy scenery of the summer stock circuit, stood directly in the path of the slowly falling wall. Stepping to the down-stage end of it, he threw his shoulder against it and gradually shoved it back to an upright position where the weight of the ceiling once more stabilized it. With a perfectly straight face and without breaking character he ad-libbed, "They just aren't building these houses as well as they used to."

This, certainly, is an excellent example of what may occur when only the love of theatre and an ability to draw recommend one for the complicated job of scenic designer. These two qualities were obviously not enough! Should they be his only qualifications, the designer is likely to find working in the theatre a frustrating, exasperating experience and one that is likely to prove prohibitively costly to producer and production alike.

What then are the prerequisite studies in preparation for work as a scenic designer? Let's take them up one by one but not necessarily in the order of their importance.

History of the Theatre

The history of dramatic production is at least 2500 years old. Each age and civilization during this span of years developed a form of dramatic expression which was acceptable in its own time and place, but differed, sometimes radically, from that which preceded or followed it. Plays chosen for production in a yearly program are selected with an eye toward variety and are likely to range from Aeschylus to Albee. Anyone seriously interested in designing for the theatre must know not only its history but its plays. He must be familiar with plays of all periods and must know and understand the staging conventions that were used when these plays were first produced. He may frequently use this knowledge to good advantage in solving the technical problems of a contemporary play by use of techniques perfected in an earlier period. Many stage conventions of earlier periods in theatre history are being revived and seem quite at home on the new stages of today.

Directing

The production of a play is a cooperative venture necessitating a close working relationship among those in charge of the various phases of work. The more thoroughly the designer understands the problems facing the director, actor, lighting artists, technician, and costumer the more intelligently he can assist in finding solutions for these problems.

Of these fields, perhaps the most important for the designer to know is direction. Ideally, this should not be a superficial knowledge picked up by watching a director at work in rehearsals or by reading a few chapters in some book on directing. Preferably this knowledge should be gained by regular attendance at a course in direction where the problems of the director are explored in depth and where the student is expected to act as a director of classroom productions. Play analysis, interpretation, mood, style, stage movement, picturization, and balance are some of the facets of a production that vitally concern the director and have a direct bearing on the final form of a setting. The more thorough and substantial his knowledge of directing is, the more easily a designer can create a scenic background that will assist in expressing the ideas of a particular play.

Acting

There is much to recommend a designer's having some experience as an actor whether he be a Garrick or a Stumblebum. He is much more apt to consider such details as steps that are too high and narrow, ramps with too steep an incline, or practical windows that are unreliable, if as an actor he has personally encountered some of the horrifying moments on stage created by poorly planned or awkwardly placed physical features of a setting. There is no substitute for such an experience and no amount of talking or reading will bring the problems into focus as clearly as personal experience.

Stage Lighting

Obviously an audience will see nothing of the designer's set until it is lighted. Stage lighting is one of the designer's most effective tools and he must know how to use it to realize its full potential. As lighting control improves and as new instruments are introduced, lighting becomes more and more important to the total visual effect. (It is not unusual to see productions in which area lighting or projections supplement scenery or even replace it.) The designer who does not understand how colored light reacts on colored pigments and fabrics runs the risk of having the color scheme of his designs unintentionally altered, sometimes with disastrous results. In educational theatre as well as professional theatre, the designer is often responsible for lighting his own productions. The need for a thorough knowledge of stage lighting should be evident.

Technical Production

Within the organization of a producing theatre no relationship between two staff members is closer than between the designer and the technician. This is not surprising since it is difficult to draw a sharp line of demarcation between the work of the two men. The process of designing and building scenery is no different from that found in any other field where an idea for an object is conceived, placed on paper as a sketch, translated into accurate mechanical drawings, and finally transformed through construction into a three-dimensional reality. The effectiveness of the designer's plan depends upon how faithfully the technician follows his specifications and dimensions. A careless or unthinking technician who decides that "a few inches variation here and there will make no difference" may do a thorough job of disturbing or destroying the proportion, line, and balance that the designer has tried to incorporate into his settings. Naturally, the designer checks the work in progress in the shop with great care and sees to it that his plans are accurately followed. He realizes that once his designs have been approved for a production, the director has every right to expect the finished setting to be a proportional enlargement of the design, not a rough approximation of it. Therefore, the closest kind of cooperation between the designer and technician is necessary.

More frequently than not in educational theatre, the work of the designer is combined with that of the technician; the two areas are the responsibility of one individual. This tends to solve the problem of faithfulness in execution, but at the same time it underlines the need for the designer to be thoroughly knowledgeable in technical production.

Students of design who are manually adept and who find working with tools no particular problem may think it unnecessary to bother with a study of technical production. However, the construction of scenery involves problems not always encountered in other types of construction. Scenery is built in one place and used in another, so it must be easily moved. For convenience in storage and shifting, scenery is usually constructed in separate pieces which must be joined and taken apart quietly and easily. It is usually finished on only one side. It must be both strong and light in weight. It must be planned so that it can be built rapidly and inexpensively. A sound knowledge of the intricacies of building, rigging, and shifting scenery cannot be ignored by those who would design in the theatre.

Costume Design

The paths of the scene and costume designers cross at several points. Understanding and accord on matters of period, style, and color are essential to achieve a sense of unity. The need for having costumes and backgrounds designed within the same period is obvious, but the need for a constant interchange of ideas between the two designers on matters of style and color requires attention. A costumer may take a narrow point of view and look upon scenery as merely a background for a parade of his costumes; a set designer may think of costumes only as color accents for his scenery. Such extreme points of view are sometimes encountered, much to the discredit of all concerned. The director, who is responsible for seeing that all elements of the production are in accord, should spot such extremism and exercise his authority to correct it. Ideally, costumes and scenery should complement each other to present a single visual effect.

Some producing organizations, in educational and community theatres, attempt to combine in one person the duties of scene designer, lighting artist, technician, and costume designer. This is a hopeless arrangement if the production schedule calls for more than two or three productions in a nine-month period. Unless the production schedule is planned for such a leisurely pace that each phase of the work can be completed before moving to the next, there simply is not time enough for one person to carry on all activities simultaneously. It is not at all strange that organizations which persist in having one person do all design and technical work for their productions are constantly looking for new personnel to replace those who have wisely escaped.

One quality which is essential in the work of a designer cannot be taught in a classroom like the six background studies we have just listed. That quality is creativeness. A candidate may draw well, he may have a background in fine arts, and he may have worked with color, line, and form, but there is still no assurance that he possesses true creativeness. Just what then is creativeness and how can it be developed? There seems to be little evidence that it can be taught in a formal way or at a scheduled time. Artistic creativeness is in part that unique quality possessed by a designer which distinguishes his solution of a given artistic problem from that found by any other designer. It is that quality in a design which sets it apart from all others as being accurately expressive of and completely appropriate for the play involved. Such work may be characterized by great simplicity of form or color, it may be based on an unusual treatment for a commonplace object, or it may depend upon the cleverness of idea or on an amusing treatment of subject matter. Be it any one of these or a combination of several, it is always distinctive in its attractiveness. For the few who possess this gift it is no trouble to design in a creative fashion; others seem to gain creativeness by dint of dogged perseverance; some, even after herculean effort, never achieve it. It may be comforting to know that some students are completely unaware that they possess a creative flair simply because they have never taken the opportunity so to express themselves.

2

AN APPROACH TO SCENIC DESIGN

The young designer who seeks to find in the theatre a medium in which he may express himself with absolute freedom is facing disillusionment. An artist in the field of graphic arts is free to express himself as he will. He may choose any subject which intrigues him and treat it in any manner and style which appeals to him. While he may find that others do not immediately appreciate his finished work, he is limited in what he does only by his imagination and the restrictions of the medium in which he works. On the other hand there is probably no field of creative work in which the artist faces more limitations and restrictions than he does in scenic design. It is well for the beginner to understand this, for unless he is willing to pit his creativeness and ingenuity against the many limitations and unless he is willing to listen to others and make adjustments in his work to meet specific requirements, he will be more contented working in some field other than theatre.

Let's look at these limitations to see how they influence a designer's work. In the first place, the subject matter is not of his choosing; the content of the play dictates it. He may disagree with the subject matter, dislike the story, feel no sympathy or interest in the characters, and hate the period in which the play is laid; yet he is expected to produce designs that are expressive of the play.

Assuming that he overcomes his aversion to the script, his designs are subject to the criticism of a director who may feel that some alterations are necessary in order to accommodate his planned stage business or to augment his interpretation of the play.

Beyond these initial obstacles there are a series of hurdles presented by each member of the production staff; the designer must clear these hurdles before his work can come to life before an audience. The technician is concerned about the elaborateness of the designs. Can they be built, painted, and rigged within the time set aside for that purpose? Can the settings be constructed in units that can be readily shifted and stored? Is the scheme of shifting practical?

The lighting artist is worried about the position of the sets on stage. How can he light them if no provision has been made to let light reach them? Must he find new mounting positions for his spotlights? What is to be the height of the bridge and teaser and does it remain constant for all settings? Can a unit of scenery which casts a heavy shadow on the cyc be changed?

The costumer is vitally concerned about the color of the settings since the costume colors are to be seen against it. If he has no choice of color because altered costumes from stock are to be used, the color scheme of the sets must be changed. Can an actress wearing a hoop skirt enter and exit through the doorways as designed? Can actors wearing high-heeled boots and carrying swords manage the steep steps the designer has planned?

The business manager is concerned with costs. Can the sets be built for $300 and, if they can't, how can they be simplified to reduce the cost? The alterations and suggestions of the production staff are evaluated by the designer. He either incorporates them into his designs or furnishes alternative solutions for the problems. The revised plans are once more presented to the director for his approval.

The beginning scenic designer is much like any other apprentice learning a complex procedure. He may feel overwhelmed by the number of factors and individuals that influence his work. However, with each completed production he gains additional knowledge and experience until it is no longer necessary to depend upon others. He gradually finds himself in the position of an established contributing member of a production staff with others as willing to listen to his suggestions and ideas as he is to theirs.

One may ask why, since there are so many limitations in the field, anyone would want to design for the stage. There is another, and a much healthier, way of looking at those prohibitions. Rather than looking upon them as limitations the designer should consider them as additional tools of his trade and capitalize upon them as such. As he masters the complexities of stage lighting, becomes acquainted with stage equipment, and learns the problems associated with costumes and budgets, he gradually learns to use them to gain effects impossible to achieve by any other means. He suddenly discovers that as an artist he possesses many more tools with which to express himself than his brother artists who are restricted to the use of brushes and pigment. This fact obviously attracts many designers to the theatre. There is also a tremendous appeal in seeing your contribution to a production come to life on stage. Your design is no longer just a sketch on illustration board nor even the usual painted scenery on stage; it suddenly becomes an intrinsic part of a greater whole. The movement of the actors, changing light, shifting color accents, all accompanied by the sound of voices, tranform a static design into a three-dimensional composition that is alive.

An asset to anyone who proposes to work within the structure of a theatrical production staff is an understanding of its organization and his relationship to other members of the staff. This is especially important for the designer to understand, not because his work is any more important than that of others, but simply because his work must be finished first. The director, technician, lighting artist, and costumer are limited, if not halted completely, in the performance of their duties until the director and the designer have completed their plans. For this reason the following sections on the elements of a production and the organization of a production staff are included.

An analysis of a successful production will reveal that it is not the achievement of any one or two individuals but the composite result of the work of a number of artists, craftsmen, and workers who have a clear understanding of the importance of their particular efforts to the total effect. Such an analysis will further reveal that a production consists of a series of elements that are irrevocably interlocked and are to be found in productions of all types.

Elements of a Production

THE PLAY, DIRECTING, AND ACTING

The nucleus of the entire production is the manuscript. The director is responsible for breathing life into the script; working through the skill of the actors, he gives to the production his interpretation of the playwright's ideas. It is the director who must synchronize all phases of the production and combine them in a manner that gives unity to the production. Although the fields of writing, acting, and directing each demand special skills and training and could therefore be classified as separate elements, they are grouped together here as one element because they are inseparably united by the one purpose of conveying the playwright's intention.

SCENERY

The element of scenery actually embraces two fields of activity—artistic and technical. The artistic field is represented by the creative work of the designer who is concerned with the problem of interpreting the script through the medium of scenic design and of creating a visual environment for the action of the play. The technical field is represented by those who are responsible for the mechanical operations of drafting, constructing, painting, rigging, and shifting of scenery. Scenery may be defined as a series of two- and three-dimensional units which are usually placed on stage to enclose, to form, or to designate the acting area. When painted, rigged, and lighted, they form the background for the action of the play.

PROPERTIES

Properties include all practical or decorative parts of the design that are not structurally a part of the setting. They fall into several classifications depending upon their size, placement within the setting, and use. Trim, as it is sometimes called, or decorative props usually serve no practical purpose other than to help the designer establish the period, nationality, and locale of the setting. They are usually placed against a wall or suspended from it. Set or floor props usually stand upon the stage floor and include all of the furniture normally used by the actors. Hand props are objects carried to and from the stage by the actors or used by them while on stage in the performance of established stage business.

LIGHTING

Advancement in the control of light and improvement in the efficiency of lighting instruments have opened a new field for creative work. The lighting artist has found that by the proper selection and placement of his lighting instruments, by the subtle use of color and intensity, he can literally "paint with light." Revelation of form, emphasis of scenic and dramatic composition, and enhancement of emotional content of the play are among the contributions a lighting specialist may make to a production.

COSTUMES

This field is as highly specialized in its own way as is that of the scene designer. The two fields have many factors in common and each includes both creative and mechanical phases of production work. The costumer strives to incorporate within each costume design features and details which are indicative of the period, the country, the social class, and the individuality of each character.

BUSINESS MANAGEMENT

Even with a subsidized theatre, one that does not depend entirely on box office income for its existence, no small part of the production work is concerned with business transactions dealing with budgets, rentals, purchasing, bookkeeping, and publicity. In professional theatre, where duties of this type are heaviest, they are usually handled by an assistant producer or a general manager. In educational or community theatre this position is usually filled by the director of the theatre or by some other member of the staff who combines this work with his other assignments.

Organization of the Nonprofessional Theatre Staff

Plate 1 illustrates the general pattern for organizing a production staff for most educational and community theatres. This plan is based upon the six elements of production previously discussed. The chart indicates a supervisor for each phase of production and lists the people working under his supervision. No two theatre production staffs are likely to be identical. Obviously, variations in the number of permanent staff members and in their particular aptitudes and abilities will force changes in a staff's manner of operation. Such a diagram must be adjusted to the personnel of each producing group. However, it is of value as a guide and as a means of checking the distribution of the work load among those responsible for specific assignments.

The various members of a theatre production staff are listed below with a brief account of the areas in which they work, their duties, and their responsibilities. It may sometimes be necessary for one person to hold two or more of these positions. This can be done effectively only with a full understanding of the duties of each position, taking into consideration when the peak work load of the combined assignments will occur during the preparation period.

AUTHOR

The author, though usually not considered a member of the production staff, is the creator of the script. When he is present during the preparation of his play, he assists the director by making revisions in the script and he may be asked to advise on such matters as characterization and interpretation.

DIRECTOR

The director is responsible for the interpretation of the play and the choice of style in presentation. With this goal in mind he plans stage movement and coaches the actors in vocal and body interpretation. He establishes a rehearsal schedule designating the times at which a particular scene or act will be rehearsed. In collaboration with the technical staff he determines the number of dress rehearsals and decides whether or not the production is complex enough to warrant additional technical rehearsals. It

ORGANIZATION OF A PRODUCTION STAFF DURING PERIOD OF PREPARATION

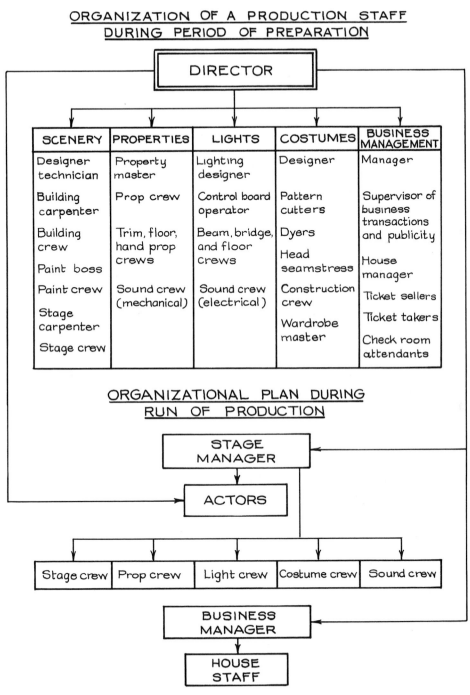

SCENERY	PROPERTIES	LIGHTS	COSTUMES	BUSINESS MANAGEMENT
Designer technician	Property master	Lighting designer	Designer	Manager
Building carpenter	Prop crew	Control board operator	Pattern cutters	Supervisor of business transactions and publicity
Building crew	Trim, floor, hand prop crews	Beam, bridge, and floor crews	Dyers	House manager
Paint boss			Head seamstress	
Paint crew	Sound crew (mechanical)	Sound crew (electrical)	Construction crew	Ticket sellers
Stage carpenter			Wardrobe master	Ticket takers
Stage crew				Check room attendants

ORGANIZATIONAL PLAN DURING RUN OF PRODUCTION

STAGE MANAGER

ACTORS

| Stage crew | Prop crew | Light crew | Costume crew | Sound crew |

BUSINESS MANAGER

HOUSE STAFF

PLATE I

is his responsibility to see that settings, costumes, props, and lighting harmonize with the acting and that all express the idea of the play. It is the director who possesses the authority to make final decisions regarding any phase of production work.

STAGE MANAGER

The stage manager is the director's right-hand man. Since the director is seldom backstage during a performance, he must delegate his authority to someone else who then assumes the responsibility for running the performances. The stage manager's duties vary considerably with different organizations and from one production to another. In professional theatre he is usually in attendance throughout the entire rehearsal period and may have some active part in rehearsing mob scenes and bit parts. In educational and community theatre he may take over his duties only a short time before final rehearsals. However, he must begin work on a production early enough to become familiar with all aspects of the production or he may not possess the knowledge required to supervise a performance. He is responsible to the director for synchronizing all backstage effects with the planned action and business of the play. He has authority over actors as well as crew members during the run of the production. On elaborate shows the stage manager may have one or two assistants.

PROMPTER

The prompter or bookholder attends all rehearsals. He aids the actors in memorizing their parts and keeps a careful record in the prompt copy of all stage business and action. An important part of the prompter's duty is the skillful feeding of lines to an actor who has "gone up" during performance. Some modern directors do not use a prompter during performance. They feel that some actors might never learn their lines if they are allowed to rely on a prompter to help them each time they have a memory lapse. Even these directors, however, may use a prompter during early stages of rehearsal and for purposes of keeping an up-to-date prompt copy. But after the time when actors are supposed to have their lines committed to memory the directors prefer to leave the actors to extricate themselves as best they can from situations resulting from forgotten lines.

SCENE DESIGNER

The designer provides the sketches for all the visual backgrounds required by a production. He is responsible for transposing his perspective sketches into mechanical drawings that describe the setting in terms of specific dimensions. These drawings, called the designer's plans, consist of ground plans, sight-line drawings, front elevations, detail and full-scale detail drawings. He may supplement his plans with a scaled three-dimensional working model of the setting. He provides the technician with the general scheme for shifting and may designate possible scenic and property storage areas. In collaboration with the director he selects all floor and hand properties. He is responsible for the final trimming and decoration of the settings.

The designer sometimes has an assistant who aids him with drafting, scene painting, and securing of the correct properties and set decorations.

PAINT CREW

The paint crew is under the direct supervision of the designer or his assistant. In educational theatre the crew usually consists of students assigned to it as a part of their laboratory experience or of volunteers who are interested in this phase of production work. All of the scenery, special effects, and built properties are painted by this crew.

TECHNICIAN

The technician is responsible for transposing the designer's plans into working drawings and for the division of the settings into units for easy construction, handling, and shifting. He perfects the designer's general scheme for shifting scenery and solves in detail the problems concerned with construction and rigging. He determines the sequence of construction in order to provide the director with those practical parts of the sets that can be used to good advantage by the actors during early blocking rehearsals. He anticipates the need for specific building materials and stage hardware and orders them in time to prevent construction delays. All stage equipment and machinery are under his supervision. With the aid of the building carpenter and stage carpenter the technician supervises the building, assembly, and rigging of all scenery. Sound effects and special properties which must be built are constructed under his supervision.

DRAFTSMAN

The technician may have one or more draftsmen to assist him in transposing the designer's plans into working drawings from which the scenery and special properties are actually made. In educational theatre, when the building schedule will permit, the drafting may be done by graduate assistants or advanced students in technical production. Since the drafting done by students must be carefully checked for possible errors and because they may not work rapidly enough to keep ahead of shop construction, the technician may do most of the drafting.

BUILDING CARPENTER

The building carpenter is the shop foreman whose duty is to supervise the actual cutting, covering, and assembling of all units of scenery called for by the working drawings. He keeps the technician advised as to the amount of building materials on hand. He assigns work to each member of the building crew and checks the progress of each unit under construction. At the request of the technician he will conduct a trial set-up of a setting to check the sizes of its various parts, to determine if the parts fit together accurately, and to see that bracing and joining hardware is correctly placed. The maintenance of all hand and power tools is under his supervision. He sees to it that the scene shop is kept clean and that all building materials and hardware are properly stored.

BUILDING CREW

The building crew is usually composed of volunteer workers or students from classes in stagecraft or technical production who work on the crew as a part of their laboratory requirement. The larger universities and colleges may have graduate assistants who are experienced in construction work and who assist in this phase of production work.

STAGE CARPENTER

In both educational and community theatre productions the duties of the stage carpenter are frequently combined with those of the stage manager. The stage carpenter is responsible for rigging, shifting, and storing all scenery during dress rehearsals and the run of the production. He plans the sequence of shifting operations, designates storage areas, and makes crew assignments. He must see that the scenery is kept in good condition during the run of the play and that settings are properly struck and stored at the close of the run.

STAGE CREW

The stage crew, like the building crew, is composed of either students or volunteer workers. Students are usually alternated from the building crew of one production to the stage crew of the next to provide them with an opportunity to learn two phases of backstage work and organization.

PROPERTY MASTER

Properties are selected by joint agreement of the director and designer. The director decides if they are suitable for planned stage business and if their appearance is satisfactory; the designer is concerned that they are of the proper period, style, and color to harmonize with the setting and the rest of the furnishings. Properties may be purchased, rented, borrowed, or built by members of the prop crew under the supervision of the technician from working drawings provided by him. Since properties are moved and stored simultaneously with the shifting of scenery, the property master and his crew work under the supervision of the technician or stage manager and in close cooperation with the stage and light crews.

PROPERTY CREW

The members of the property crew, under the direction of the property master, help to procure or construct all props. During the rehearsal period and the run of the play the crew is usually divided into two sections, one responsible for placing, shifting, and storing all decorative and hand props, the other responsible for floor props. In order to save time and to prevent possible loss or damage to small hand properties carried by actors, one or two crew members may be assigned to collect the props from the actors as they leave the stage after each scene.

SOUND CREW

Ordinary off-stage sound effects of a simple nature are usually handled by members of the prop crew. Most modern theatre plants have high fidelity sound systems equipped to handle those productions calling for a great many varied and complicated sound effects or to furnish recording for those scripts that are accompanied in part by music. In such cases it is advisable to have a special crew that can devote its entire attention to synchronizing the sound effects to the action and business of the play.

LIGHTING SPECIALIST

The lighting specialist collaborates closely with both the director and the designer in planning the lighting of a production. In many theatre organizations the duties of the lighting artist are combined with those of the designer. These duties include making a light plot, determining the number and types of instruments to be used, placing and mounting these instruments, setting up the control board, and developing a control board cue sheet.

LIGHT CREW

The work to be accomplished by the light crew logically divides the crew into sections responsible for specific duties. (1) The control board operators, under the direction of the lighting artist or designer, work out the most efficient set-up of the board and plan the cue sheet. They also operate the board during rehearsals and performances. (2) The floor crew is in charge of all lighting instruments mounted on or within the setting or placed in off-stage areas which can be reached from the stage floor. Such instruments include tower spots, horizon strips, backing lights, table or floor lamps, and fireplace effects. The floor crew is responsible for the proper placing and focusing of these lights, for the use of correct color mediums in them, and for handling them during scene shifts. (3) The bridge crew controls the focusing of spotlights and the changing of color mediums on all instruments on the bridge and controls any special effects mounted on the bridge. (4) The beam crew, usually consisting of only one or two members, has charge of instruments mounted in the beams, in the side wall coves of the auditorium, or along the balcony front.

COSTUME DESIGNER

The costume designer submits sketches to the director for all costumes to be used in the play. These may be rented or made in the theatre's shop. If they are to be made, the designer usually submits material samples and cost estimates with his sketches. After the director approves the designs, the costume designer determines what stock costumes may be altered for reuse in the current production. He then buys the remaining fabrics and accessories and supervises the making of the costumes. When costumes are rented, the designer places the orders and supervises the adjusting and fitting of the costumes after they are received.

COSTUME CREW

The costume designer usually divides the members of his crew into two groups, construction crew and wardrobe crew. The construction crew is concerned with the actual cutting, fitting, and assembling of all costumes. The wardrobe crew assumes responsibility for the completed costumes and their maintenance from the time they are first used in dress rehearsal until the close of the run. Productions calling for numerous or fast costume changes may need another division of the costume crew—the dressers. Dressers assist the actors in dressing and in arranging various parts of the costume, wig, and accessories.

BUSINESS MANAGER

The business manager keeps the books and accounts of the organization. Cost estimates for costumes, scenery, properties, and lighting are submitted to him by production supervisers; and he sees to it that costs are kept within established budgets. It sometimes becomes necessary to simplify or alter some phase of the production work to bring the total cost within the limits of these budgets. Changes made for this reason must be approved by the director, and notification of such changes must be given to the superviser whose work is affected by them. All production expenditures, requisitions for new materials, petty cash accounts, and rental charges are countersigned by the business manager. A running total account of the production cost is easily kept in this manner. All advertising, news stories, and general publicity are handled by the business manager after consultation with and approval of the director. Working under the direction of the business manager is the house staff, whose duties are sufficiently described by their titles: (1) house manager, (2) ticket sellers, (3) ticket takers, (4) ushers, (5) cloakroom attendants, and (6) parking lot attendants.

Need for Cooperative Effort

Over a hundred individuals might be involved in the production of a single play such as G. B. Shaw's *The Devil's Disciple*. When it is realized that many workers perform their duties without contact or consultation with other staff members and that the first opportunity they have to see the combined result of their efforts is the dress rehearsals, it becomes apparent that their supervisors must be aware of the work being done by other parts of the staff and must share a common goal with them. With an organization as large and as complicated as a theatre production staff the need for close cooperation among all area supervisors should be obvious. Without it misunderstandings can occur or differences of opinion may not be resolved in time to prevent their affecting some vital part of the work. This could well result in a performance in which some elements of the production show a jarring lack of accord.

Cooperation among members of a production staff can best be achieved by complete understanding achieved through conferences at which problems bearing on the production are discussed. Such meetings should occur frequently enough during the preparation of a play so that those who are responsible for various phases of the work are conscious of the progress made by others and are aware of any changes that may affect their own work. In this manner many problems which might go unnoticed until the first dress rehearsal can be caught early and solutions found for them. The time thus saved during the dress rehearsal period can well be devoted to the integration of the elements of a production rather than to the correction of needless mistakes resulting from lack of communication.

A well-balanced artistic production is achieved only when all area supervisors and their various assistants have a complete understanding of the ultimate goal to be attained by the fusion of their individual efforts.

3

THE DESIGNER'S PROCEDURE

There is no set of rules governing the procedure a designer must follow in creating the designs for a play. Each scenic artist develops a method suited to his own manner of working, and this method may differ radically from that of another designer. However, there are factors common to all productions which must be considered by the designer regardless of his individual manner of working. It makes little difference in what order he gives them his consideration just as long as he gives them the attention they deserve and finds workable solutions for the problems they present. The following outline lists the salient points which must be recognized in the procedure of designing for the stage:

1 Analysis and interpretation of the play
2 Production staff conferences
  a. Requirements of the director
  b. Style chosen for presentation
3 Technical demands of the play
  a. Number of settings
  b. Shifting problems
  c. Actors' requirements
4 The stage and its equipment
  a. Size and shape
  b. Storage space
  c. Shifting facilities
  d. Lighting equipment and facilities

5 The shop and its equipment
   a. Relationship of shop to stage
   b. Size and shape
   c. Available power and hand tools
   d. Storage areas
   e. Stock scenery available for reuse
6 Sight lines
   a. Relationship of auditorium to stage
   b. Vertical sectional sight-line drawings
   c. Horizontal sectional sight-line drawings
7 Research
   a. Source material on which designs are based
   b. Historical background for play's action
8 Sketch or model
   a. Compositional requirements
   b. Adapting source material to designs
9 Designer's plans
   a. Ground plans
   b. Front elevations
   c. Detail drawings
   d. Full-scale detail drawings
10 Selection of properties
   a. Floor props
   b. Hand props
   c. Decorative props
11 Scene painting
12 Trimming and decorating the assembled setting

Analysis and Interpretation of the Play

An artist cannot interpret a play in terms of design after only a casual reading. He must have a thorough understanding of the script before he can hope to talk intelligently with the director regarding matters of style and presentation. He should read the play through once for the plot and general idea. He must understand the mood of the play, its characters, and their relationship to each other. This first reading will establish in the designer's mind the period in which he will work, the country and the locality where the play is laid, and the type of characters and individuals who are to inhabit the background he will provide for them. These first impressions are very important to the designer as they give him the general emotional quality and tone which he will attempt to convey by his designs.

The second reading of the script should be for the purpose of noting any special demands of the action upon the scenery. For example, there may be a window that must be raised or lowered, a door that must be battered in, an alcove in which an important bit of business must be played, or special items of furniture that are spoken about in the dialogue. Frequently key lines in the dialogue give important suggestions on the manner of decoration, the condition, or the furnishings of a room. In preparing an episodic play, one with many scenes and settings, it is advisable to make a chart of the sequences of scenes at this early stage. In productions of this type it is difficult to keep in mind the correct order of scenes. Frequent references to such a chart during the preliminary planning, particularly in regard to the scheme of shifting, will help eliminate mistakes that would later prove difficult to correct.

When given a play to design, many students or inexperienced theatrical workers make the mistake of not doing their own analysis first, but turn immediately to accounts and photographs of other productions of the same play. Rather than helping a designer the impressions gained from such a study make it extremely difficult for him to do creative work of his own.

A second common mistake stems from the student's desire to execute faithfully every suggestion made by the author regarding the setting. Frequently it is impossible to do this simply because the physical limitations of the stage the designer happens to be working on will not permit it. Yet there are those who insist on a slavish adherence to the playwright's written word in spite of all limitations imposed by lack of space, money, or equipment. The result may be a setting which not only does not reflect the character and atmosphere suggested by the playwright but does not even replace them by any original contribution of the designer. Under such circumstances the only sensible solution is a complete break from the text, adapting the setting to the requirements of the stage on which it will be produced. This may result in a setting radically different in form from that proposed by the playwright, and yet the new form may incorporate those qualities he sought to achieve. Fortunately many playwrights recognize the ability of the designer and they suggest in just a few words their own ideas of the setting. The actual arrangement of the room, the location of doors and windows, the placement of furniture, and similar details are left to the judgment of the director and the designer.

Of course, the author's description of the setting should not be ignored, but it is important for the student to realize that there is often more than one possible arrangement of a setting and that frequently the designer will find a more satisfactory solution for his particular stage than the one proposed by the script. It has been this author's experience in working with established playwrights that they are remarkably reasonable men. They are not upset because the designer did not follow the written description of the setting to the letter; they are really concerned with but one thing, that their plays be given the most suitable and expressive backgrounds that circumstances will permit.

Production Staff Conferences

The first production staff conference on a new play is extremely important to all area supervisors. It is at this meeting that the general approach to the play will be determined. It may be that the designer has formed an idea concerning the interpretation of the play which is at variance with that of the director, or that the designer and the costumer have chosen styles which cannot be successfully combined. Obviously, a clear understanding must be reached and a single point of view must be settled upon to insure a unified and artistic production.

James Bridie's *Tobias and the Angel* as produced at the University of Iowa may be taken as an example of the importance of decisions made at an initial production conference and their influence on the manner of presentation. The play, a fantasy, calls for five settings: Tobit's hovel in Nineveh, the banks of the Tigris, Raguel's house in Hamadan, a khan near Kifri, and a lane in Nineveh outside Tobit's hut. T. W. Stevens was a visiting guest director who, because of previous commitments, did not arrive on the campus until shortly before rehearsals were to begin. This precluded the possibility of early staff conferences. Although it was recognized as a risky procedure it was thought that some time might be saved if the designs were completed before Mr. Stevens's arrival. These were then submitted to him at the first production meeting. Fortunately he found the basic designs acceptable. However, he suggested that the fragile plot of the story should not be interrupted between scenes by the usual opening and closing of a curtain, that all scenery should be shifted in full view of the audience. The production was to be so planned that after the initial opening of the curtain, the audience was to behold, through a decorative false proscenium on an otherwise barren stage, the kneeling figures of six brown-clad slaves before whom stood the imposing figure of an overseer holding aloft a large cymbal. At a crash of the cymbal the slaves were to scurry offstage and immediately reappear guiding or rolling before them units of scenery that when assembled formed the setting for the first scene. The strike of one scene and the assembly of the next was to be conducted in a similar fashion until the closing of the front curtain signified the end of the play.

This one suggestion of the director, that the scenery be shifted in view of the audience, had a marked influence on other phases of the production. The designs, by Louis MacFarland, were rearranged to adapt them to the new scheme of shifting. The technician devised unusual methods of construction and joining so that all parts of each setting either rolled into place or were lowered into position from the grid. Lighting instruments were mounted and prefocused in position to avoid any delay in lighting after the sets were in position. Additional costumes were needed for the slave stage-hands and extensive rehearsals were required before the scene shifts were perfected to be quick and seem effortless. The whole effect was well worth the additional effort as it accomplished what the director had hoped for. There was no interruption in the telling of the story and the shifts became a part of the play that the audience seemed to enjoy almost as much as the story.

No two directors are likely to approach the first production meeting with the same experience, philosophy of direction, or manner of working. A director who is perhaps uncertain of himself in the field of design may give a script to the designer with some such comment as, "See what you can do with this." This approach may be all right if the designer is experienced, but it's hardly helpful unless he is. At the other extreme is the director who brings to the first production meeting a predetermined ground plan for the setting; he may even have chosen a color scheme and specified the furniture arrangement he would like to use. Agreeing with such a director simplifies the work of the designer, but at the same time it makes it difficult to do original work or interest the director in what may well be a better set of designs. Somewhere between these two extremes is found the ideal working relationship between the director and the designer; each understanding the problems and difficulties of the other and each willing to make concessions for the sake of the better staging of a play.

Discussed at this first meeting are other factors bearing on how the designs will be treated. These include the length of time remaining before the opening of the production, what part of the budget has been set aside to cover the cost of scenery, the stage on which the play is to be mounted, and the equipment and facilities available for the handling of settings.

Technical Demands of the Play

The play requiring one or two settings is not likely to present any major technical problems which must be solved before the designs for its settings can be completed. As a matter of course the designer will note any practical features about the settings such as French doors through which a wheel chair must be rolled or a stair balustrade over which an actor must vault. It is in the play of many settings that technical demands may force the designer into a method of staging different from any he has yet employed. It may be that the play under consideration has eight or ten settings or that two or more scenes with their separate backgrounds are seen simultaneously. With plays of this type finding the proper technical solution makes the difference between a production of merit and one that is lost in a maze of delays and interruptions.

The episodic play, with its many settings and its elaborate technical demands, is becoming common in the work of many contemporary playwrights. Designers are constantly being forced to new heights of imagination and ingenuity to find technical solutions and styles of design that satisfactorily express the intent of the plays. Frequently the answer is found in the simplification of the sets, by allowing one or two focal objects to stand for the whole; or the problems may be solved by the use of extremely ingenious methods of rigging and shifting more realistic backgrounds. Another avenue of attack on such problems is the employment of a staging convention taken directly from the history of drama. Sidney Howard's *Yellow Jack* was superbly handled on a mechanized adaptation of the Elizabethan stage. The Second Moscow Art Theatre capitalized on the characteristic features of an early Italian Renaissance stage for their spirited production of *Twelfth Night*. The designer of the Siminov Theatre in Moscow used three small revolving discs, a device introduced to the theatre by the Greeks, in mounting a play with six settings on a stage of extremely limited dimensions. As long as plays remain as varied in form as they are today, as long as theatre stages differ as radically in form, size, and equipment as they now do, there can be no standardization in the types of problems a play may present in production or in the answers found for its staging. The production of each play has its own distinctive problems that the designer, and frequently the entire production staff, may be called upon to solve.

Many theatre organizations throughout the country unfortunately tend to avoid plays that require more than the usual one or two settings. Any play which makes what at first seem to be excessive technical demands is automatically shunned as being too difficult or too expensive to produce. This decision is often reached without first having tried to find a possible scenic solution. In many cases these plays could be produced with satisfaction, and perhaps even with distinction, if the production staff were willing to abandon their usual realistic approach and to employ a new and seldom used staging convention.

Production methods which the author observed on a tour abroad, particularly in the Soviet Union, made this point remarkably clear. Many of the theatres there had extremely limited stage space and equipment, yet time and again elaborate productions in these theatres were triumphs of scenic ingenuity. The directors and designers were apparently willing and eager to experiment with new production methods and as a result there was a distinctive creativeness associated with the production of their plays that was definitely refreshing.

Of significant help to a designer is his ability to recognize the restrictions placed upon him by the method that will be needed to shift the scenery he is planning. The method of shifting should be considered an integral part of his plan of design and not an extraneous element to be confronted for the first time after the settings have been assembled on stage. When speed is needed in scene changes, a designer who understands the difficulties accompanying the shifting of elaborate and complicated scenery will frequently alter his plans in order to utilize a more rapid and easier scheme.

The Stage and Its Equipment

Perhaps the one external factor which influences the designer's work more forcefully than any other is the stage and its equipment. Variety in the types and sizes of stages is infinite, ranging from the temporary stage erected on the high school gym floor to the large, well-planned and well-equipped university, municipal, and commercial stages. Each theatre has its own advantages and disadvantages which make it unlikely that a production planned for one could be moved to another without making adjustments in the size of the proscenium opening, in the masking, or in the manner of shifting.

It is mandatory that the designer possess full and accurate information about the stage on which his settings will be mounted if he is to avoid embarrassing or costly mistakes that can impair the success of a production. A list of the information he should have can be compiled by answering the following groups of questions.

1 What are the extreme limits of good sight lines from the auditorium to the stage? From the balcony to the stage? At what height must the teaser be placed to assure those in the balcony a full view of the stage? At this teaser height can those in the front row of the orchestra see over the top of the cyc? Will additional masking be necessary?

2 What are the dimensions of the orchestra pit? What type of pit is it—open, trapped, or elevator? Where and how is access to it made?

3 What is the shape and size of the apron? What is the relationship of the apron to the proscenium arch? What access is there to the apron other than through the front curtain? Are there stairs from the orchestra level to the apron or proscenium doorways by which it can be reached? What are the sizes and the locations of these?

4 Is it possible to vary the proscenium size by a rearrangement of the tormentors and teaser? What is the placement and size of these masking units? Can they be adjusted easily?

5 How does the main curtain operate—fly, draw, or tab? Where are the controls located? How far upstage of the proscenium is the curtain line? How much off-stage space is required for storage of the curtain when it is in an open position?

6 What is the distance from the light bridge to the curtain line, tormentors, and teaser? Is the height of the bridge adjustable? What are the dimensions and weight capacity of the bridge?

7 What is the location and what are the dimensions of the locking rail, storage areas, stairways, fire doors, dressing rooms, switchboard, electrical floor pockets, floor traps, radiators, fire-fighting equipment, and other backstage facilities?

8 What type of flying system does the theatre possess? How many battens are there and where are they placed? Is there any variation in the length and capacity of the battens?

9 What is the relation of the cyclorama to the acting area and to off stage storage room? Is there danger of fouling the cyc when the battens are raised or lowered?

10 Can stage screws be driven into the stage floor? Is it necessary to remove the floor cloth to use a floor trap? How far does the floor cloth extend off stage beyond the limits of a normal setting?

11 What type of electrical control board is there? What is its capacity? Where is it located—backstage, in the rear of the auditorium, or in the balcony? How many and where are the electrical outlets on stage? What permanent positions are there for mounting lighting instruments?

12 What, if any, is the size, location, and method of operation of permanent scene-shifting equipment such as wagon stages, jackknife stages, slip stages, or built-in revolves?

The Shop and Its Equipment

Any designer-technician who has fought with the limitations imposed on him by a scene shop that is far from the theatre, too small, poorly equipped, or on a floor level different from the stage is the first to acknowledge how much these facts influence his work.

The ideal shop for the educational and community theatre is large, well-equipped, adjacent to the stage, and on the same floor level. Unless the scene shop meets these specifications it can force alterations in the designs, it can complicate the manner of construction, and it can add to the time needed to rig scenery once it reaches the stage. Since scenery is one of the costliest items in a production, the designer must know what materials and scenery are kept in stock and are available for reuse. He should also be aware of the location and accessibility of the storage areas for this stock.

Sight Lines

The sight lines of a setting may be easily determined once the exact form of the setting has been fixed by the designer's ground plan. Two drawings are required to show all of the possible lines of vision from points in the auditorium to the setting in its position on stage. These two drawings are called the horizontal section and the vertical section. The horizontal section is used in checking how much of the width of a setting can be seen from different positions in the auditorium and in determining how long various masking units must be when placed at given distances from openings within the setting. The vertical section is used in establishing the teaser and bridge height and in checking how much of the vertical faces of the set can be seen from different positions in the auditorium. It is also used in determining the height of all masking units. (The subject of sight lines will be treated in greater detail in Chapter 8.)

Research

One need choose only half a dozen plays at random to learn how varied the settings are as to period, country, and locality. Without first doing some research on the matter, very few designers would be able to recall from memory the characteristic architectural features, typical furniture arrangements, or color schemes of, say, an eighteenth-century Norwegian inn or an Italian villa of 1870. The need for research is apparent.

The beginner will find it easier to arrange interesting and satisfactory settings once he has acquired a working knowledge of the forms on which his designs must depend. Obvious as this fact may seem, many students attempt to design settings without first consulting any source material. The time spent by an artist in becoming thoroughly familiar with the architectural and social conventions of the period on which he will base his designs is usually well repaid by the added character and depth of his finished work. It is well to remember that an audience depends upon the setting for the visual atmosphere of the play just as much as it depends upon the acting and direction for the interpretation of the characters and story.

The field from which a playwright selects the setting for the action of his play is much too wide and varied for anyone to attempt a systematic listing of all possible source materials. Many designers, however, compile a catalogue of pictures and drawings clipped from rotogravures, magazines, newspapers, and travel brochures of subject matter that may prove helpful. Their files will also contain lists of books and periodicals with good illustrations of especially interesting architectural forms, period furnishings, or other details. These files, or morgues, as they are usually called, contain pictures on a wide range of subjects including interesting room arrangements, unusual exteriors, fireplaces, window treatments, decorative fences and walls, furniture, color schemes, paintings, tapestries, antiques, stained glass, or anything else that the designer may at some time find useful.

A partial list of the types of books that most frequently prove helpful would include those on the history of architecture, ornamentation, interior decoration, antiques, period furnishings, and travel. It is well for the beginner to understand that source material is the nucleus of the finished design.

Sketch and Model

The designer's creative ideas must be transferred to some medium that will permit him to convey them clearly to all members of a production staff for their information and possible criticism. One of two methods is normally employed. He may present his ideas in the form of a colored perspective sketch or he may prefer to use a scaled, three-dimensional model.

The perspective sketch usually represents the setting as it would appear on stage to a spectator who is seated in the orchestra level about halfway back in the auditorium. The sketches are generally quite complete; they represent the true form of the setting and give a clear indication of the furniture and property arrangements. If possible, they also include some suggestion of the desired lighting effects.

Certain types of designs do not lend themselves well to interpretation through the medium of two-dimensional sketches. While not ordinarily used in planning a simple production, the model is extremely helpful when more clarity is needed. It often helps in working out the intricacies of a complicated shifting technique involving numerous settings. When the setting is highly irregular in form, as would be the case with the mountaintop in *High Tor*, a model makes it easier to perceive the form. If the designer must concern himself with problems associated with forced or faked perspective, a model provides a simple means of visualizing the results of his efforts.

Models must be made to scale. They may be constructed of cardboard reinforced with tape and strips of wood or they may be made of modeling clay. The cardboard models are used chiefly for illustrating interiors or working out the details of scene shifts, while the clay models are most often used advantageously to show the form of irregularly shaped exteriors.

Designer's Plans

The process of designing for the stage is in no way finished with the completion of the water-color sketch. Matters of proportion and balance, the relationship of architectural details, and the establishment of definite dimensions are clearly as much a part of design as the rendering of the sketch. A well-executed perspective sketch is quite adequate in describing the general appearance of a proposed setting, but in one respect it is completely unsatisfactory. There is no way of incorporating within the sketch the necessary dimensions and specifications required by the technician in building the setting. To a lesser degree the same is true with a model. Although models are built to scale, it is difficult to inscribe all the required dimensions on their various areas, and in some cases it may be impossible. In such cases a technician can get the dimensions directly from the model by applying a pair of dividers to it and then reading the distance on a scale rule, but this process is at best not too accurate because of the small scale used in the construction of most models. Consequently, the designer accompanies either his sketch or model with a supplementary series of mechanical drawings describing the setting in terms of actual feet and inches and giving all specifications and information necessary.

The designer's plans usually consist of ground plans, front elevations, detail drawings, full-scale drawings, and in some cases, sight-line drawings. Each of these drawings will be discussed at length in Chapter 8, but for the present the following descriptions will suffice. A ground plan is a scaled top view of the setting showing its relationship to the auditorium and to the stage on which it will be used. It indicates the exact position of each part of a setting and specifies the length or width of each individual member. The front elevation is a scaled mechanical drawing representing the front view of the setting as it would appear when drawn in a single plane. All vertical dimensions are indicated on it. This drawing supplements the information contained on the ground plan.

Some features of a set, such as the details of a fireplace or the different parts of an elaborate stairway, cannot be shown clearly on the elevations because only one view of them is seen and because the scale used in the drawing is too small. In the elevations the designer can establish the over-all size and shape of such details by their relationship to the surrounding wall areas and other architectural features, but their small size prevents him from describing them clearly. Most three-dimensional units of a setting are re-drawn to a much larger scale and may be represented by two or more views accompanied by the necessary dimensions and notations. These drawings are called the detail drawings. The intricate nature of some features, such as wallpaper patterns or the design of a bannister, may be so exacting that the designer draws them to full scale, that is, they are drawn life-size. In productions where masking problems are a major consideration, the technician and the lighting artist are each provided with a set of sight-line drawings.

The designer's mechanical drawings provide him with his first opportunity to check his design after the size and form of its various parts has been established. He has the comforting feeling of knowing that if he approves of what he sees in his drawings he will also approve of the completed set since it will be a proportional enlargement of the same ideas translated into building materials.

The drafting of the designer's plans is a step in the process of designing that can seldom be accomplished by anyone but the designer without an excessive waste of time. Even experienced draftsmen, accustomed to working with a particular designer, can only guess at the proportions and dimensions the designer has in mind, draw them up, and then submit them to the designer for his corrections and approval. Consequently, most scenic artists find it faster and easier to do most of the drafting themselves.

Selection of Properties

During the period required for the construction of the scenery the designer has time to turn his attention to the matter of selecting the furniture, draperies, and pictures used in dressing the finished set. The design of the setting may be clever and original; its construction, painting, and lighting may be excellent; yet the total effect can be severely damaged by poorly selected properties. Both designer and director are vitally interested in this step. It's the designer's responsibility to see that the properties chosen are as distinctive as circumstances will permit and that they are of the correct period and color to harmonize with the tonal quality of the setting. The director, while interested in these same qualities, is primarily concerned that the properties be suitable for the stage business planned around them. When a particular property cannot be purchased, rented, or borrowed, it is constructed in the scene shop from plans submitted by the designer.

Scene Painting

In both educational and community theatres the setting is invariably painted under the close supervision of the designer. Because of the inexperience of his paint crew, he may even do much of the painting himself. Realizing the importance of a good paint job to the over-all appearance of his settings, he is vitally concerned with the quantity and hue of mixed pigments, the correct blocking-out of areas to receive given colors, the proper techniques of application, and the careful blending or shading of different colors. Even in the commercial theatre, where this phase of production work is done by professional scenic painters, the designer is present at the studio in an advisory capacity. If union regulations prevent him from helping with the actual painting, he will supply those in charge of the painting with color charts, graphs, and samples in addition to the regular colored sketch.

Trimming and Decorating the Assembled Setting

The final step in the designer's procedure is trimming and decorating the completed setting after it has been assembled on stage. This is more a matter of adjustment than anything else, provided the preliminary work has been carefully planned. The rug is laid, the furniture and decorative props are placed in position, all wall hangings are affixed, and for the first time the entire setting with all its trim can be seen as a single unit. It is the exception to find a setting that does not need some adjustment of properties. A property which is unsuitable for the planned stage business or an upholstery color which conflicts with costume colors under stage lights will force last-minute adjustments.

4

REQUIREMENTS FOR A WELL-DESIGNED STAGE SETTING

Throughout the history of drama we find that the importance attached to the backgrounds against which plays have been presented has varied greatly. Plays have been given without scenery of any kind or they have been presented on bare platforms backed by a simple drapery. They have been presented before architectural backgrounds and on stages with a few suggestive screens serving to identify the place of action. At other times the attention paid to scenery has been out of all proportion to its value to the play; the play was just an excuse for a dazzling display of spectacular scenic inventions.

Producers in the twentieth-century theatre, with the exception of a few radical experimenters, have shown a sensible appreciation for the value of all elements of a production and have succeeded in coordinating them so that no one element is allowed to dominate. Every effort possible is made to keep the lighting, scenery, properties, and costumes in accord with the direction and acting in order to create a unified production.

In view of the part that scenery plays in the successful production of a play, a thorough understanding of what is meant by scenic design is essential. Stated simply, scenic design may be defined as the art of creating an expressive and appropriate environment for the action and characters of a given play. Although there may be many exceptions to a listing of the requirements a well-designed stage setting must meet, it is nevertheless true that most good stage designs have complied with the majority of the requirements listed below.

1   The setting must be expressive
 a.   Of the play, its mood and spirit.
 b.   Of the historical period of the play.
 c.   Of the nation or country where the action is laid.
 d.   Of the locality or part of the country where the action is centered.
 e.   Of the strata of society from which the characters are chosen.
 f.   Of the season of the year.
2   The setting must be based upon the elements of good composition—the arrangement and adjustment of color, line, form, and mass for the sake of harmony, sequence, and balance.
3   The setting must be practicable.
 a.   It must meet the needs of the director's planned stage business.
 b.   It must be serviceable to the actors who use it.
 c.   It must meet the technical demands of the production—rapid construction, easy shifting, and proper storage.
 d.   Its cost must fall within the limits of an established budget.

Expressive Setting

THE MOOD AND SPIRIT OF THE PLAY

No set of rules can be formulated to apply with equal success to the designs for all settings. What may prove correct and suitable for one play may be misleading and injurious to another. However, there is one requirement for a successful design that is not likely to meet with an exception: the setting should be expressive of the play for which it was designed. The style of the design makes little difference. It may be realistic, suggestive, or stylized, but it must always reflect the mood and spirit of the play. Even reconstructions of certain types of architectural stages, those that do not attempt to portray a particular place of action, can be made expressive of the play. They can suggest the period in which the dramatist worked by capitalizing on the architectural peculiarities and the staging conventions of the time. The popularity of Shakespearean plays presented on stages of this type with a minimum of scenic effects attests to the expressiveness and success of this treatment of design.

The expressiveness of a design depends less on faithful use of source material than on the designer's ability to incorporate something in his work that is suggestive of the emotional characteristics of the play. The mood and spirit of a play are the basis for design. The mood of a play is its dominant emotional quality. The spirit usually refers to the manner in which the acting and the direction of the play are handled. To use an obvious example, suppose that an old melodramatic play is being considered for production. The play has many situations that are essentially serious and depressing; some of the characters would normally elicit sympathy and pity from an audience. Melancholy, sadness, and despair seem typical of the general emotional tone or mood of the play. However, rather than emphasize these qualities, which might appear amusing to a modern audience, the director chooses to change the entire emotional tone of the play by the manner or spirit in which the play is to be interpreted and directed. Stress is laid on any comic elements, and the serious and dramatic situations are exaggerated in the acting and directing to a point where they become insincere. The mood of the play thus changes from one typified by sadness and depression to one of lighthearted amusement. The designs should, of course, reflect these same qualities. For the original mood the settings might be seriously and accurately realistic in terms of the period of the play. For the play as reinterpreted by the director, the settings might be satirical and exaggerated, portraying in an amusing and pictorial fashion the same spirit of overemphasis and insincerity that is evident in the acting and directing.

THE HISTORICAL PERIOD OF THE PLAY

The period in which a play is laid affords the designer an opportunity to use source material to add character, interest, and expressiveness to his designs. One need only walk through the streets of his own city comparing different types of private dwellings and business houses to appreciate what a difference just a few years will make in the style and treatment of these structures. The great variation in the appearance of the exteriors, the changes in building materials, the manner of working with the materials, the differences in ornamentation and color all represent only a short span of years taken from the total history of architecture. If so many variations are apparent within a short period of time, one begins to appreciate what they can encompass when observations are extended to cover architecture in all countries and all times.

Styles in the planning of homes and business concerns change almost as rapidly as the fashions of the clothes that man wears. This may not be due so much to man's conscious desire to seek a new architectural style with which to express himself as it is to the changes in living requirements brought about by new means of transportation, new methods of heating, new work habits of the population, and all the other factors that change social patterns.

Even more noticeable than the differences in the style and form of exteriors of period homes are the differences in fashions of arranging and decorating the rooms within them. It is only necessary to mention some of these items to bring to the student's attention an appreciation of their value to a stage setting. It may be that the form of the room itself may prove interesting. Are the ceilings high or low; the walls plain and unadorned or broken by interesting window arrangements, recessed bookcases, and ornamental niches? Is the fireplace built into the wall or does it project out into the room? What are the characteristic features of the fireplace itself? The wall surfaces of a room may provide the designer with just the features he needs to make his setting distinctive. Are they composed of rough logs or boards, or are they made of plaster and finished with wainscoting and decorative wallpapers? Perhaps there is an unusual type of baseboard and chair rail or there may be a plate rail, some type of cornice, or a beamed ceiling. Other architectural features of a room that are well worth the designer's closest attention are such items as the shape and construction of unusual window arrangements, ornamental window and door casings, the patterns formed by the muntins of the windows and the paneling on the faces of doors. No designer is likely to overlook the possibilities offered by distinctive lighting fixtures such as an elaborate chandelier, wall brackets, or candelabra.

In furnishing a room the designer is confronted with a bewildering choice of material. Care should be exercised to prevent the settings from becoming cluttered with too many pieces of furniture that are used simply because they happen to be of the right period. Five or six carefully selected pieces usually suffice, especially when they are supplemented with the proper decorative props. Decorative properties include those furnishings which serve no specific purpose in the business of the play but which seem desirable for the dressing of a set. Decorative props usually include several carefully selected small pieces of furniture, such as an ottoman, occasional chair, or wall table, and all pictures, wall hangings, lamps, lighting fixtures, and similar articles.

Too often the stage floor remains the same uncompromising dull brown of the regular floor cloth regardless of the type of setting placed on it. This is understandable when sight lines are such that few people can see the stage floor or when theatres are operating on limited budgets, but it is difficult to justify otherwise. The designer should consider the floor covering as the foundation of his color scheme and should give to it the consideration such an important part of his design should have. A special muslin or canvas floor cloth is not very expensive and it can be repainted for use in a number of productions. It can be painted to suggest an earthen floor, or a floor made of flagstone, tile, rough planking, decorative wood, or linoleum. It may even be painted a solid color to represent over-all carpeting.

NATIONAL ARCHITECTURAL CHARACTERISTICS

Before the turn of the century and the introduction of television, foreign aid, and air freight there was a distinctive quality in the style of architecture used by different nations. At the present time there is a sameness in archi-

47936

tectural treatment that makes it difficult to distinguish an apartment house in
Sweden from one in Buenos Aires or New York City. Except for the signs
printed in a foreign language a street scene in Chicago might closely resemble one in modern Tokyo or London. When the period of a play permits
it, a designer should be quick to include any distinctive national trait or
feature that will give added character to his design. The farther back one
moves in time the more this national difference in architectural styles becomes apparent. Man's religion, his background, his associations, his eco-
nomic standing, the climate in which he lived, and the availability of building
materials all influenced the form of his architecture. Selection of information
from an authentic source is an obvious necessity for an expressive setting.

LOCALITY

A full appreciation of the enormity of the differences in architectural
styles is reached when one realizes that within a given period and country
these changes are multiplied many times over by the matter of geographical
location. One might take as an example three typical farmhouses in the
United States about 1880. The small farmhouse of a struggling New England
farmer was compact, built for warmth to withstand the rigors of a bitter
winter. In order to avoid trudging through the snow from one building to
another the house was joined directly to the sheds, outbuildings, and sometimes even the barn. This is vastly different in style from the flimsy house
of a tenant farmer in the deep South. His major concern was in building
a house that would be cool in hot weather. His home was built on piles
to obtain better circulation of air beneath it. Frequently the house was
divided into two sections joined by a roofed but unwalled breezeway in
which meals could be served in hot weather. Again to avoid the heat, meals
were cooked on an open fireplace in the yard or on a fireplace located in
a section of the house separated from the bedroom by the breeze-way. The
ranch house of the old West was an even more primitive dwelling. It was
sometimes built with no floor other than earth and it often contained only
one or possibly two rooms. The walls were constructed of logs chinked with
clay and the roof of sod or hand-hewn shingles.

STRATA OF SOCIETY

Most stage settings, except completely unrealistic designs, give the
audience some indication of the type of characters who are to inhabit the
settings. The designer normally uses the properties and furnishings as tools
in achieving this effect and on occasion he may use the actual form of the
room to help tell the story. Certainly this would be the case with such an
obvious example as the zany walk-up apartment in Neil Simon's *Barefoot in
the Park*. The color scheme, the selection of furniture and trim, the manner

LEWIS–CLARK
NORMAL SCHOOL
LIBRARY

of arranging them within a room can do a great deal to give some indication of the type of person who lives there. A living room inexpensively but tastefully furnished will suggest one type of occupant, while the same room, expensively but gaudily furnished will most certainly lead an audience to expect the occupant to be an entirely different type of individual.

While this may seem a small item in the matter of design, its importance can be brought into focus when one realizes how much a person's opinion of another may change after visiting his home and seeing the taste, or lack of it, expressed in its appointments. There are, of course, many exceptions and many situations that will prevent the designer from giving any indication as to personalities or the level of society from which the characters are taken; but when the circumstances will permit, it is another step that the designer can take toward making his setting expressive of the play.

SEASON OF THE YEAR

One of the author's experiences may serve to point out the importance of the designer's giving close attention to the properties he selects to establish the season of the year. The setting was the front porch of a house in Indiana during early spring. At one corner of the porch was a large lilac bush in full flower; backing the porch swing was a trellis covered with a climbing rosebush, also in full flower. The fact that lilacs and climbing roses do not flower at the same time in Indiana, if anywhere, unfortunately escaped the notice not only of the designer but of the entire production staff. It remained for a sharp-eyed member of the audience to call this obvious mistake to the attention of an embarrassed designer.

There are not many physical features of a setting that can be used to establish a season of the year. The designer might resort to the use of screened doors and open windows to suggest summer or to a view through storm doors and windows of a snow-covered landscape as an indication of winter; but normally he depends heavily on costuming, stage lighting, and hand properties to establish the season.

Elements of Good Composition

This is the one step in designing for the stage that an artist will take almost unconsciously. The elements of composition remain the same no matter what area the artist has chosen as a field for expression. The sculptor working in wood or marble, the easel painter with oil pigments and canvas, or the scenic artist with his water colors and illustration board are all concerned with the adjustment of color, line, form, and mass for the sake of a composition that is orderly, well arranged, and unified. As an artist, his whole background has been centered upon and concerned with studies involving the different aspects of composition. By nature and training his eye and mind have been taught to appreciate subtle relationships of space and form; he enjoys working with color and in finding harmonious color combinations; he is intrigued by proportion; and he takes pleasure in adjusting various elements of his design to establish a sense of balance and stability. It is no wonder that this phase of the designer's work does not need to be underscored; he simply thinks this way and it seems only natural that he should so express himself.

The principles of good composition are simple. They are harmony, sequence, and balance achieved through the proper adjustment and relationship of color, line, form, and mass. Harmony means the sense of blending, the feeling of agreement, the sense of unity that is obtained when all elements of a design are in accord. Harmony can be developed by imparting an interdependency to the various parts of a design and by avoiding contrasts that that are too startling. The recurrence of similar forms and ideas or a manner of treament that characterizes an architectural period may be taken as a manifestation of harmony. It is a recurrence of particular patterns in each of them that distinguishes Colonial furniture from Elizabethan, and Louis XIV from either of the others. As a term, harmony is used in a much broader sense than either sequence or balance; as a matter of fact, it may embrace one or the other or even both of these terms.

Sequence refers to that quality of having an orderly, logical interrelationship of successive parts; it is the logical progression of a salient feature through all parts of a composition. Applying this definition directly to the field of scenic design it may be considered as the order of placing physical features of the composition according to their value in such a manner that it leads the eye to the dominant or focal point of a setting. This sense of progression should not only be evident within the composition of a single setting but should be manifest in the kinship of designs employed for all the settings of a given play.

Balance can be established within a design by the adjustment of color, line, form, and mass in a manner that will impart a sense of stability or repose. Balance may be symmetrical or asymmetrical. Symmetrical or geometric balance is the arranging of objects of similar tone, size, and shape equidistant from a central point. This type of balance is extremely obvious and very easy to establish, but, because of its obviousness and its lack of interest, most scene designers do not make extensive use of it. This is not to imply that symmetrical balance must be avoided at all costs. There are occasions when the nature of the play or the manner of its direction make the use of symmetrical balance mandatory. Such was the case with a production of Euripides' *Medea* designed to suggest the formal arrangement of a Greek theatre and with a production of Oscar Wilde's *The Importance of Being Earnest* that was given completely symmetrical settings because the director felt that they would help emphasize the artificiality of the play and the stilted manners of the times.

Asymmetrical balance, variously called occult, informal, or hidden balance, is a little more difficult to appreciate but its use on stage is much more extensive. Here the balancing is done partly by the eye and partly by the mind. Objects of different color, form, and scale may be arranged in an asymmetrical manner and yet give the effect of perfect equilibrium or balance. The balancing of such a group of dissimilar objects in a composition depends primarily upon their arrangement in relation to each other and upon their differences in emphasis due to their tone, position, measure, and shape.

It must be realized that the success of a scenic design does not depend upon the composition as it appears in the final color sketch, but must be judged by its appearance after it has been transformed into three-dimensional scenery, painted, rigged, and properly lighted. Production elements may add to or detract from the effectiveness of the design depending upon the degree to which the designer has considered them. A stage setting is never a static composition. It varies with the color and intensity of the lights upon it. Color emphasis and harmony shift with the movement of actors, and the movements of the actors also affect the balance of a design.

There are four basic elements in a composition—color, line, form, and mass. These may be considered the actual tools of the scenic artist; what he does with them will determine how effectively he expresses the environmental idea of a play.

Color is probably the best known and the least understood of these four elements. We grow up with color all about us and accept it without thought; we use it in our daily life without being really conscious of it. Although we depend upon it in many ways, people who have not made a special study of color would probably be at a loss for words in trying to discuss it. A man will usually try to describe a color by comparing it to another color that can be seen at that time or he will use what he hopes is a descriptive phrase: "It's about the color of your tie but not quite so blue" or "It's just exactly the color of lemon yellow." Even the manufacturers of household paints give their products descriptive names such as seafoam green, old ivory, battleship gray, or fire engine red. These terms may be quite satisfactory for the general public, but not for those who must work closely with color and must describe it accurately.

Any color has three qualities that may be used in describing it—hue, saturation, and brilliance. Hue is the distinctive quality of a color that differentiates blue from blue-violet, yellow from yellow-orange, or purple from red-purple. Hue is simply that quality which allows us to distinguish one color from another. Saturation refers to the vividness or strength of a hue as opposed to neutrality or gray. For instance, the hue alizarin crimson is fully saturated as it comes from a tube of water color pigment; nothing can be added to it to increase its strength. The degree of saturation may, however, be lowered by adding to it varying amounts of its complementary

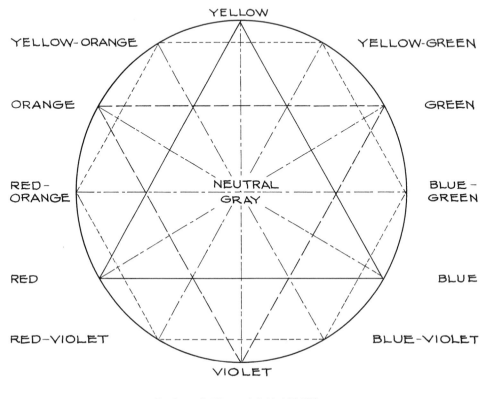

YELLOW

YELLOW-ORANGE   YELLOW-GREEN

ORANGE   GREEN

RED-   BLUE-
ORANGE   NEUTRAL   GREEN
                   GRAY

RED   BLUE

RED-VIOLET   BLUE-VIOLET

VIOLET

COLOR   WHEEL

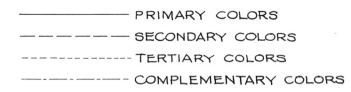

———————————— PRIMARY COLORS
— — — — — — — SECONDARY COLORS
- - - - - - - - - - TERTIARY COLORS
—·—·—·—·— COMPLEMENTARY COLORS

PLATE 2

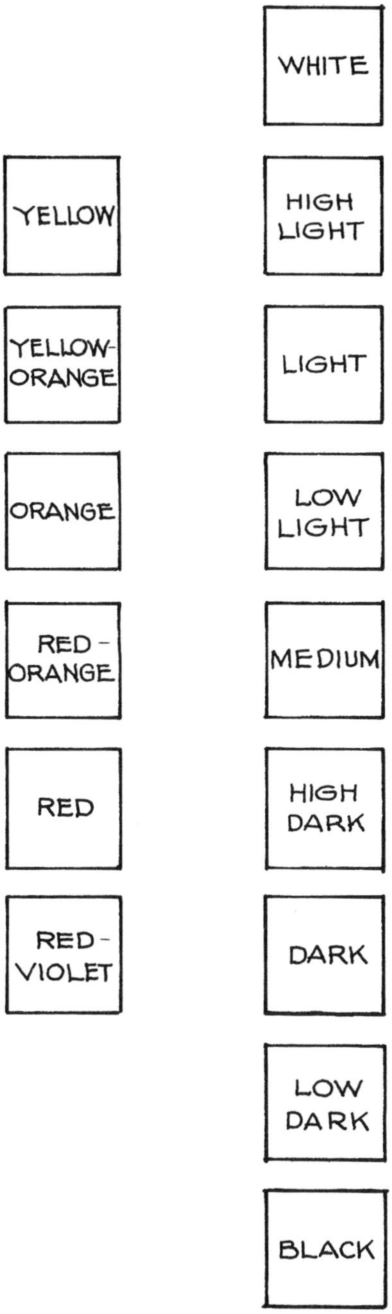

	WHITE	
YELLOW	HIGH LIGHT	
YELLOW-ORANGE	LIGHT	YELLOW-GREEN
ORANGE	LOW LIGHT	GREEN
RED-ORANGE	MEDIUM	BLUE-GREEN
RED	HIGH DARK	BLUE
RED-VIOLET	DARK	BLUE-VIOLET
	LOW DARK	VIOLET
	BLACK	

SCALE OF BRILLIANCE COMPARED
WITH SATURATED PRIMARY, SECONDARY,
AND TERTIARY COLORS

PLATE 3

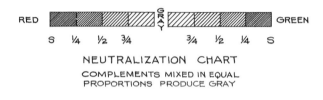

NEUTRALIZATION CHART
COMPLEMENTS MIXED IN EQUAL
PROPORTIONS PRODUCE GRAY

PLATE 4

hue. Complementary hues are the hues directly opposite each other on the circumference of a color wheel. When equal amounts of two complementary hues are mixed together neither hue predominates, resulting in a gray or what is called complete neutrality. Brilliance is that quality that distinguishes the lightness or darkness of a hue. Webster's *New Collegiate Dictionary* calls it "the degree of resemblance to white or difference from black." It is that attribute of a hue that permits us to distinguish between a light blue-green and a dark blue-green (see Plate 3).

Three other words often employed in working with color are tint, shade, and tone. Each of these words has a precise meaning and there is little reason for their being misused as frequently as they are. A tint is formed when a hue is raised toward white by the addition of a white pigment or, in the case of transparent water color, just clear water. A shade is formed when the hue is lowered toward black. Tone is used to describe the combined results of what has been accomplished with hue, saturation, and brilliance.

This account of the qualities of color and the terms used in describing them can be better understood if they are studied with the drawing of a color wheel (see Plate 2). The principles of color demonstrated by this diagram apply both to the transparent water colors used in rendering sketches and to opaque scene paint.

It should be apparent that the student cannot learn to use color just by reading about it. The more he paints and experiments, the more charts he makes, and the more he drills, the sooner he will learn to solve the problems of laying a smooth wash and the sooner he will master the tricks used in different painting techniques. With this acquired skill he will find that the time required for rendering a sketch is noticeably reduced and that rendering has become a step in designing that is both pleasurable and satisfying.

There are any number of excellent books dealing with color theories, color harmonies, and rendering in water color. The students who have a special interest in this area are advised to seek out some of these books. Dr. Ladd-Franklin's book on *Colour and Colour Theories*, M. Luckiesch's *Color and Its Application*, Walter Sargent's *Enjoyment and Use of Color*, and Arthur Guptill's *Color in Sketching and Rendering* are but a few of those that will prove helpful.

The remaining three elements of composition—line, form, and mass—are no less important than color as tools of the designer's trade. They have the advantage of being less complicated in nature and certainly easier for the beginner to understand. As line is used in artistic terminology it can be said to be a mark made by a pencil or brush and forming a part of a formal design. These marks form the boundaries between areas of different colors and are used in describing the shapes of objects represented. Line is capable of infinite variation; it may be straight or curved, horizontal or vertical, diagonal or jagged. It may also be a combination of two or more of these types. Line in some form is used in every design that is placed on stage. Since line is so essential to all design, the artist has learned certain truths about its use. The exclusive use of one type of line creates a design that has complete unity, that is, all of its parts seem to belong together, but the result is apt to be tiresome and monotonous. Two types of lines used in equal measure are likely to be as monotonous in effect as the exclusive use of one. Interest is added to a design by varying the types of lines used, and variety is as essential to good design as unity. However, the indiscriminate use of a variety of lines leads to confusion. Therefore, the best designs invariably have one kind of line predominating, with variety achieved by the tasteful introduction of lines of different kinds.

The boundary or contour line of an object describes its form. We learn to distinguish one object from another in many ways; we may recognize it because it has a distinctive color or because its texture is unlike anything else, but principally we distinguish one object from another because of its form. Form and shape are synonymous when used in this context. The form of many objects can be described by comparing them to geometric figures such as a square, a triangle, a circle, or a rectangle.

Mass is the cubic area occupied by an object. Solids of any form have width, height, and depth. When a solid is placed on stage so that a spectator can see all three dimensions, the spectator is much more conscious of the solid's mass than when he can see only one or two dimensions. Occasionally the term mass is used to describe the effect produced by a series of objects arranged or grouped so closely together that they are not seen as separate objects but as a composite whole. For example, in a cluster of trees the shape and mass of each tree is less well defined and less important than the shape and mass of the whole cluster.

The Practicable Setting

A stage setting may be perfectly expressive of the play, cleverly and beautifully designed, and yet fail to be completely satisfactory. A designer, elated at finding especially rich source material or enthusiastic about an original design, may lose sight of the fact that his setting must be practical. Ignoring this aspect of design risks the success of a production.

The four steps necessary in making a setting serviceable may seem obvious, but the frequency with which they are overlooked testifies to the need for additional comment.

THE NEEDS OF THE DIRECTOR

Frequent conferences between the director and the designer are the answer to problems arising in this area. Consequently, the form of a set and the relation of properties to it are closely watched by a careful director. As a further precaution, many directors request that the position and form of a setting, along with the location of the more important properties, be marked out in chalk or tape on the stage floor during the early rehearsal period. Frequently such a procedure results in the discovery of needed changes at a time when the changes can easily be made in the shop. This method also introduces the actors to the exact size and shape of a setting long before the first dress rehearsal, and it permits them to adjust to the limitations of a set and to establish accurately the timing of their movements and stage business. There is an additional bonus for this manner of working; it reserves dress rehearsal time for its intended purpose, namely, synchronizing and polishing all the elements of a production.

THE NEEDS OF THE ACTORS

The needs of an actor in his use of a set are different from the director's needs in planning stage business. The position and size of a doorway may be planned for some specific business the director had in mind, but what concerns the actor is "will the thing work?" Nothing is more disconcerting to an actor, or more amusing to an audience, than a door that unexpectedly and stubbornly refuses to open due to misalignment or to faulty latching hardware. Equally amusing to an audience is watching an actor attempt to crawl through a window that will not stay open and so traps various parts of that very discomfited actor. Incidents like this can have a shattering effect on an actor. His peace of mind is a critical part of any production; he has every right to expect that the mechanical parts of a setting will operate as planned and that his person will be reasonably safe in the performance of any business assigned to him.

THE TECHNICAL DEMANDS OF A PRODUCTION

Some students are not aware of the great influence the technical demands of a production may have on the work of a designer. The designer who loses sight of the fact that his designs must be planned to permit rapid and easy construction may find that there isn't adequate time to get his scenery ready by the opening of dress rehearsals. If his settings have ornate or complicated features, he should consult the technician concerning their construction. Lack of proper tools and power equipment, working space, or skilled personnel could mean that more time would be required in construction than is permitted by the work schedule.

The portability of scenery is a big factor in the ease and speed with which the scenery can be shifted. Portability is often obtained by the breakdown of a setting into sections to facilitate speedy and easy handling. This breakdown not only adds to the convenience of shifting; it is equally helpful in solving the problem of storing a setting when it is not in playing position on stage. The responsibility for the general scheme of shifting belongs essentially to the designer; but to work out the details of handling a particular unit of scenery he should consult with the technician early enough in the planning stage so that changes can be made in the designs if they are deemed necessary in order to simplify a shift. Breaks between scenes of an act for the purpose of shifting scenery must candidly be acknowledged as interruptions to the story of a play. Therefore, any steps that can be taken to reduce the time required for this purpose are steps toward greater continuity for a play.

Before the plans are sent to the shop for construction, they should be discussed with the lighting artist to determine if adequate space has been allowed for the mounting of instruments and to make sure that such instruments can be properly masked, focused, and operated from the planned mounting positions. This procedure is particularly helpful when the nature of a setting is something other than the usual living room interior. A setting with a low-beamed ceiling or with an unusually deep-roofed porch may necessitate special supporting and masking members for lighting instruments. Productions that make extensive use of light, as would be the case if projections were to replace the use of constructed scenery, must be planned in great detail and in close cooperation with the lighting artist. This is necessary to ensure satisfactory sight lines and to guarantee an unobstructed area free of suspended scenery or battens between the projector and the reflecting surface of the drop or cylorama on which the projections will be thrown.

COSTS

Sometimes the designer's "creative flight of imagination" may lift him so far above the world of reality that he loses sight of the fact that it will cost money to translate his idea into scenery. Educational and community theatres operate on budgets so restricted that most producers in commercial theatres could not even consider starting production on such terms. As frustrating as it may be at times, this condition is not without some entries on the credit side of the ledger. It places a premium on ingenuity and it encourages the use of experimental forms in design. These sometimes have a quality of freshness about them that would not have been found had unlimited funds been available.

5

MECHANICAL DRAWING

No matter what language is used, the spoken word is totally inadequate to describe a complicated object with enough clarity and accuracy to ensure its construction without error. However, a solution for this problem has been found in the universal language of drawing. Diagrams, freehand drawings, and perspective sketches can be used to give a clear, general picture of what a proposed structure should look like, but even they are not accurate enough to indicate exactly the intended size and proportion of the completed structure. To meet this need another type of drawing was developed—mechanical drawing.

As the name implies, mechanical drawing is a style of drafting that involves the use of an instrument, such as a T square, triangle, or compass, in drawing each line. It is further distinguished from freehand or perspective sketching in that the object drawn is carefully described by different views and accurately represented to scale by allowing a fraction of a foot to equal 1 foot. Providing different views and drawing to an exact scale provide a method of describing the precise dimensions and shape of an object. These drawings, when accompanied by their specifications (notes specifying the building materials, textures, or special effects to be used), give the technician a complete description of an object. Nothing is left to guesswork; he knows the exact form and size of the completed whole, he knows the form and size of its separate parts, and finally, he knows how these various parts are fitted together.

The importance of mechanical drawing to the scene designer cannot be overemphasized. After the completion of his perspective sketch, he must describe his design by another method that will permit him to represent its various parts with exact dimensions. Mechanical drawing is the method he will use. This is one of the most critical steps in the realization of a successful stage design. Many excellent design ideas have failed to materialize when transferred to scenery and paint, simply because the designer did not know how, or would not take the time, to give this phase of designing the attention it deserves. Why any designer would think of omitting this operational step is hard to understand since it provides him with an opportunity to check his design. He knows that mechanical drawings represent his setting in exact proportional reduction, and if he approves of what he sees in them, he will also approve of the completed setting. Another advantage of this operational step is sometimes overlooked; it is much easier and less expensive to correct a mistake on paper than to correct it in the shop after it has been transferred to building materials.

Drafting Materials and Instruments

For the type of mechanical drawing used in scenic design the drafting materials and instruments need not be either extensive or expensive. Such a list would include a drawing board about 20″ × 26″, a good T square with a shaft long enough to reach across the length of the drawing board, one 8″ 45° triangle and one 10″ 30–60° triangle, a pencil compass, an architect's scale rule, an eraser, drafting pencils numbered either 2H or 3H, and drafting tape.

All drafting instruments can be purchased individually from any well-stocked dealer, but a student seriously considering specializing in design will find it less expensive to purchase a complete set. Specialized instruments, beyond those contained in a set, can be bought as the need for them arises.

For classroom work a good-quality detail paper is acceptable. This comes in sheets about 18″ × 24″ and may be purchased by the single sheet. It is a heavy, opaque paper well suited to pencil drawing and will withstand many erasures. However, most production drawings are made on one of the many types of tracing paper. Drawings on this type of paper can be duplicated easily by blueprinting (white lines on a blue background) or by the Ozlite method (black lines on white).

DRAWING BOARD

The size of the drawing board is not too important provided it is large enough to accept a drawing representing the dimensions of an average stage drawn to a scale of ½″ = 1′-0″. The board is made of white pine with the ends cleated to prevent splitting. The edges of the board must be absolutely straight so that the head of the T square will ride evenly on them. If drawings are to be made on tracing paper, the face of the board should be padded with a single sheet of detail paper permanently taped into position. The padding not only makes the drawing easier to see, but also prevents sharp pencil points from cutting the tracing paper or scoring the board.

T SQUARE

The accuracy of a mechanical drawing depends to a great extent upon the condition of the T square. All horizontal lines are made by placing the head of the T square over the edge of the drawing board and guiding a pencil along the upper edge of the T square. Vertical lines are drawn by placing the base of a triangle against the T square shaft and guiding a pencil along the vertical edge of the triangle. Obviously if the head of the T square is not firmly attached to the shaft at a true right angle, neither vertical nor horizontal lines will be accurate. Treat the T square with the care that should be given a precision instrument. Do not store it by standing it on end in a corner of a room or by laying it across a radiator; the blade will warp. Hang it up by the hole provided in the end of the shaft. Take every precaution possible to avoid nicking the drawing edge of its blade, which is easily damaged. The author once interrupted a spirited game of polo being played by two students who were using their T squares as mallets and an Art-gum eraser as a ball. Needless to say, their drawings were none too accurate!

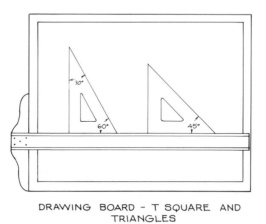

DRAWING BOARD - T SQUARE AND
TRIANGLES

TRIANGLES

Triangles may be purchased in many different sizes, but the two already mentioned, the 8″ 45° and the 10″ 30–60° triangles, are ideally suited for scenic work. Since they are used for drawing all vertical lines, triangles any smaller than these necessitate shifting both T square and triangles to a new position in order to draw a long vertical line. By placing one triangle against another and guiding both by a T square, angles of 15° and 75° can be

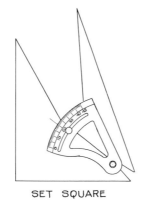

SET SQUARE

drawn. Other angles are measured by a protractor or a set square. The set square is an adjustable triangle with two parts joined by a plastic protractor reading from 0° to 45°. A threaded bolt and thumbscrew permit the two halves of the triangle to be locked at a desired angle.

COMPASS

A compass, preferably one with a lengthening bar, is needed for drawing circles or arcs. The lengthening bar, an attachment which fits into one of the compass arms, is used in drawing circles that have a large diameter. The compass can be converted into a pair of dividers (used for dividing a line and transferring dimensions) by a second attachment, a needlelike point, that replaces the lead-gripping head. Small circles or arcs are easily drawn with a bow compass. The two arms of the bow compass are made of spring steel so shaped as to force the arms apart. A threaded bar fitted with a knurled ring at its center engages both arms, makes the compass easy to adjust, and ensures that it will hold a given dimension without variation. Still smaller circles

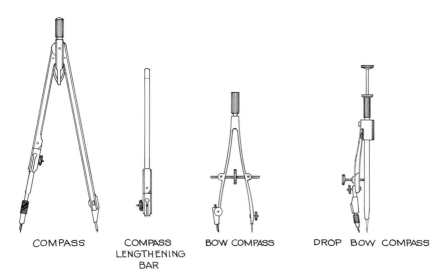

COMPASS   COMPASS   BOW COMPASS   DROP BOW COMPASS
LENGTHENING
BAR

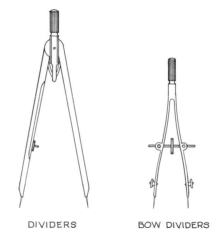

DIVIDERS   BOW DIVIDERS

are best drawn with a drop bow campass. The pivoting needle of this instrument is elongated and it slips up and down inside the pivoting shaft of the
compass. The other arm of the drop bow compass can be adjusted, like the
bow compass, by a threaded bar and knurled ring. The pivoting shaft is
fitted at the top with a concave disc on which the tip of the index finger rests;
the compass is rotated by the thumb and middle finger of the same hand.

ARCHITECT'S SCALE RULE

The key to making all scaled mechanical drawings is the use of an
architect's scale rule. An object too large to be drawn full scale on a sheet
of paper is represented by a drawing that is proportionally reduced in size.
This is accomplished by allowing a fractional part of a foot to represent a
full foot. The different scales found on an architect's rule make this process
practically painless.

The architect's rule is made in two shapes—triangular and flat. The triangular rule (which is the less expensive one) has a standard foot measure,
with each inch divided into sixteenths, and ten different scales, two on each
of the remaining five edges. These scales are:

$$3'' = 1'\text{-}0''$$
$$1\tfrac{1}{2}'' = 1'\text{-}0''$$
$$1'' = 1'\text{-}0''$$
$$\tfrac{1}{2}'' = 1'\text{-}0''$$
$$\tfrac{3}{4}'' = 1'\text{-}0''$$

$$\tfrac{3}{8}'' = 1'\text{-}0''$$
$$\tfrac{1}{4}'' = 1'\text{-}0''$$
$$\tfrac{1}{8}'' = 1'\text{-}0''$$
$$\tfrac{3}{16}'' = 1'\text{-}0''$$
$$\tfrac{3}{32}'' = 1'\text{-}0''$$

The flat rule may be a little more convenient to use, but it has only eight
scales, two on each of its four edges. (The $\tfrac{3}{16}''$ and $\tfrac{3}{8}''$ scales are missing.)

The different scales are indicated by the proper numerical figure placed
opposite its scale near the end of the rule. Find the $1''$ and the $\tfrac{1}{2}''$ scales;
both are on the same edge of the rule. Turn the rule so that the numerals
of these two scales can be read in the usual fashion, from left to right and
right side up; the $1''$ scale will be to the left and the $\tfrac{1}{2}''$ scale to the right. At

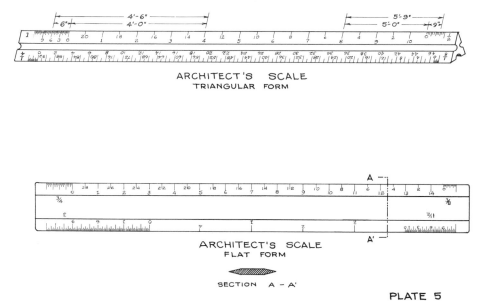

ARCHITECT'S SCALE
TRIANGULAR FORM

ARCHITECT'S SCALE
FLAT FORM

SECTION A - A'

PLATE 5

the extreme left of the 1″ scale, a space of 1″ has been divided into twelve even spaces representing inches and each inch has been further subdivided into quarters by graduated lines. The space between the o and the figure 6 to its left represents 6″; the space between the o and the 9 represents 9″. Any fraction of a foot can thus be measured. The 1″ scale reads from left to right and is marked consecutively from 1 to 10. Notice the position of the o on this scale. It is placed so that the inches read to the left of the o and the feet to the right. This arrangement makes it possible to measure a distance such as 4′-6″ without moving the rule once it has been placed on a drawing. Counting to the right of the o, place a mark opposite the figure 4. Since the inches are read to the left of the o, a mark opposite the figure 6 literally adds 6″ to the 4′-0″ dimension. The distance, then, between the figure 4 and the figure 6, on the opposite sides of the o, represents a total distance of 4′-6″.

The ½″ scale (the figures nearest the edge of the rule) reads from right to left. At the extreme right of the rule is a ½″ space that has been divided into 12 spaces representing inches, with each inch subdivided into halves by shorter lines. Fractional parts of a foot must be measured by using the different length divisional lines. Foot measurements are in multiples of two; they read o, 2, 4, 6, etc. Odd numbers, not indicated by a numeral, are found by using the marks of the 1″ scale, which fall midway between the numerals of the ½″ scale. On the ½″ scale the foot measurements are read to the left of the o and the inches are read to the right. Practice in handling a rule will make a beginner adept at finding measurements on any scale.

DRAWING PENCILS

The degree of hardness or softness of lead used in drawing pencils is designated by letter and numeral. These range from the very softest at 5B, through medium firm at HB, to 9H for the hardest lead. Most drafting for scenic work is done with pencils marked 2H, 3H, or 4H. Softer leads leave a blacker line, but they smudge easily and both the draftsman's hands and his drawing instruments are soon covered with graphite. A long sharp pencil is essential for accurate drafting. To sharpen a pencil, cut the wood from the pencil to expose about a quarter inch of lead; then sharpen the lead by rubbing it on a fine sandpaper block until it is pinpoint sharp.

ERASER

A soft, pliable, pink eraser such as the A. W. Faber-Castell Techno-tone is best for correcting penciled mistakes. It removes all graphite without discoloring or damaging the paper. An Artgum eraser is used to clean up a drawing after it is completed. Powdered eraser is sometimes sprinkled on a drawing while it is being drafted. The movement of the T square and triangles over these particles keeps the underside of the instruments clean and prevents a graphite "shadow" from forming on the paper.

DRAFTING TAPE

Drafting tape has replaced thumbtacks for holding paper in place on a drawing board. It can be quickly and easily applied, it does not protrude above the face of the board enough to interfere with the movement of a triangle or a T square, and it will not disfigure the board with a series of holes. In mounting paper on a drafting board make sure that it is properly aligned or the horizontal and vertical lines will not be parallel with the edges of the paper. Proper alignment of the paper is done with a T square. Center the paper on a board and adjust it until the upper edge of the paper is parallel with the T square shaft. Use 2″–3″ strips of drafting tape to hold down the four corners of the paper.

Drafting Symbols and Conventions

Drafting has been made easier to do and easier to read by the use of commonly accepted drafting symbols and conventions. While some of the symbols have been carried over from the fields of engineering and architectural drafting, others have been developed to meet the special needs of theatre work. Several types of lines are used in drawing. Each type of line is used for a specific purpose and should not be used for anything else. The different types of lines used in mechanical drawing are given below.

Margin line.   A heavy, solid line used as a border or to subdivide a plate when several unrelated drawings are grouped together.

Construction line.   A medium-weight, unbroken line used to outline the shape or form of an object.

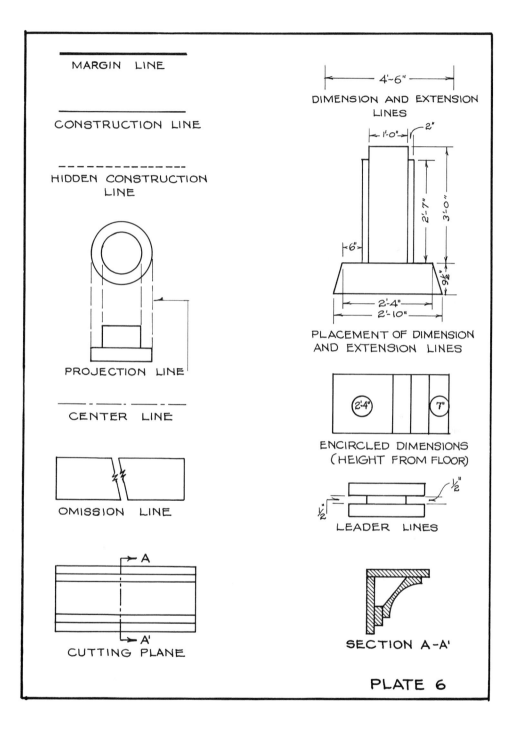

MARGIN LINE

CONSTRUCTION LINE

HIDDEN CONSTRUCTION LINE

PROJECTION LINE

CENTER LINE

OMISSION LINE

CUTTING PLANE

4'-6"

DIMENSION AND EXTENSION LINES

1'-0"   2"

2'-7"   3'-0"

6"

2'-4"
2'-10"

PLACEMENT OF DIMENSION AND EXTENSION LINES

2'-4"   7"

ENCIRCLED DIMENSIONS (HEIGHT FROM FLOOR)

$\frac{1}{2}$" $\frac{1}{2}$"

LEADER LINES

SECTION A-A'

PLATE 6

Hidden construction line. A medium-weight line of evenly spaced dashes used in describing the shape of some part of an object not visible in the given view.

Extension line. A lightweight line placed at right angles to a surface or a part of an object to show the terminal points of a dimension. The extension line is separated from a construction line by a slight space.

Dimension line. A lightweight line extending between extension lines and terminating in arrowheads. A space is left in the center of the dimension line for the insertion of a dimension. Dimensions are usually placed on a drawing so that they may be read from left to right or sideways from bottom to top. No specific instructions can be given for the placement of all dimensions, except to say that they should be placed where they can be read easily and where they will not obscure construction lines.

Encircled dimensions. Used on the ground plan of a setting to signify the height above the stage floor of a particular unit.

Leader line. A lightweight, angular or curved line, terminating in a single arrowhead, used for spotting a dimension when there is insufficient space on the drawing for conventional dimension and extension lines.

Projection line. A lightweight line of evenly spaced long dashes showing the relationship of alternate views of the same object.

Center line. A lightweight line of alternate long and short dashes indicating the center of an object; frequently used in scenic work to show the center of a stage.

Omission or break line. A medium-weight line interrupted at intervals by angular breaks; used to indicate that a part of an object has been omitted from the drawing.

Cutting plane. A medium-weight line broken at intervals by short double dashes and terminating in directional arrowheads; used on drawings where it is necessary to show a cut-away or sectional view of a structure.

Sectional shading. Lightweight, evenly spaced lines, drawn at a 45° angle; used to shade the exposed face of a sectional drawing.

Any explanatory notes accompanying a mechanical drawing must be printed. This is a precaution against mistakes that can arise from trying to read illegible handwriting. The advantage of lettering is twofold; it can be done rapidly and there is little chance of misreading even poorly formed letters. There are many styles of lettering—some very decorative and ornate, others much simpler in form. The alphabet most frequently used in mechanical drawing is called single-stroke gothic. The width of line used in forming the letters is made by a single stroke of a pencil or pen, and each letter is formed by a series of straight lines or a combination of straight and

curved lines. Either the vertical or the inclined form of this alphabet may
be used. The beginner will probably have less trouble with the vertical
alphabet since it is easier to keep the vertical shafts of the letters parallel.
Examples of the upper and lower cases of both alphabets are given in Plate 7.

The ultimate purpose of mechanical drawing is to describe an object so
accurately that no mistake can be made in understanding what was intended.
Little purpose is served in making a set drawing if the dimensions are so
badly written that they can be misread. Most of us are careless in writing
numerals; we make little distinction between the numerals 6, 8, and o or
between 7 and 9. Pay particular attention to the formation of the numerals
shown in Plate 7, one numeral cannot be mistaken for another. Remember
that misreading a dimension in the scene shop can result in a costly waste
of manhours and building materials.

ABCDEFGHIJKLMNOPQRSTUVWXYZ
abcdefghijklmnopqrstuvwxyz

ABCDEFGHIJKLMNOPQRSTUVWXYZ
abcdefghijklmnopqrstuvwxyz

1234567890
¼"   ½"   ¾"

PLATE 7

Drafting Techniques

For all practical purposes a piece of drafting paper has but two dimensions
—width and length. The basic problem facing a draftsman is representing
a three-dimensional object on a piece of paper that has but two dimensions.
If an object has only two dimensions, width and height, there is little problem. The two dimensions are scaled off and an outline drawing is made that
will describe its shape accurately. However, with a three-dimensional structure, which has depth as well as width and height, the problem becomes a
bit more complicated. The draftsman solves this problem by representing
the structure in a series of related views, usually top, front, and side views.

Several different drafting techniques have been developed to accomplish this purpose—orthographic projection, isometric drawing, oblique drawing, and cabinet drawing.

ORTHOGRAPHIC PROJECTION

Did you ever watch a prospective buyer look over a large piece of furniture? He inspects it from all angles. He backs off to look at the front, moves to look at first one side and then the other. If space will permit, he inspects the back as well. If the piece has drawers, they are slipped in and out; perhaps one is removed for closer inspection. Orthographic projection does exactly the same thing for a draftsman; it provides him with a means of describing an object by representing it as it would appear when seen from different views.

A definite relationship of one view to another and the arrangement of the views permits the draftsman to indicate the depth of an object as well as its width and height, and to do so on the limits of his two-dimensional drawing paper. The easiest way to understand this is to imagine an object, for example, a lamp table, enclosed in a transparent box with each of its sides hinged so that the box can be flattened out. Suppose that we look down on the top of the table through the box. The width and depth of the table can be seen but not its height. If we project lines from the four corners of the table to the top plane of our box and connect these points with lines, we have an accurate drawing of it. Drawings of the front, sides, and back can be projected to the corresponding planes of our box in a similar manner. When the box is unhinged and flattened out, it is two-dimensional in form as is our drawing paper. However, the different views of the table are represented in their correct relationship to each other. Notice that each drawing of the table represents it as though the observer were exactly at right angles to it. He can see no more than one face of the table at a time. For this reason, several different drawings are required to describe it completely.

A little time spent in studying the diagrams in Plate 8 should clarify the relationship of one drawing to another. This arrangement of views is the basis for all orthographic projections.

ISOMETRIC DRAWING

Most of the designer's drafting will be done by means of orthographic projection. However, for greater clarity, he may need to supplement these drawings with a pictorial sketch. Isometric drawing provides the designer with a fast and easy way of doing this without becoming involved with perspective. Two additional advantages of this technique of drafting are that three views of an object can be represented in a single drawing and that certain of its lines can be measured.

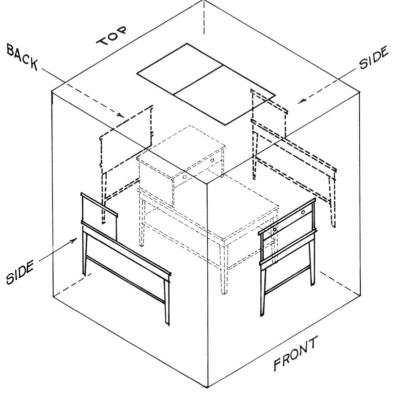

ORTHOGRAPHIC   PROJECTION

TOP

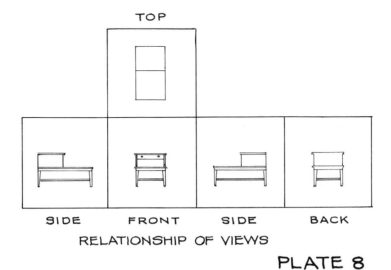

SIDE   FRONT   SIDE   BACK

RELATIONSHIP OF VIEWS

PLATE 8

Assume that an isometric drawing of a cigar box is needed. The box can be held below eye level and then rotated and tilted into such a position that one corner is closer than the others to the observer. In this position three faces of the box are visible. When the box is held in this position, its vertical edges are foreshortened. However, the isometric drawing ignores the effects of foreshortening and the vertical edges are drawn at their true lengths.

Isometric drawings are based on three lines representing the edges of a rectangular solid held in the position described above. These are called the isometric axes. Dimensions can be measured at their true length along any of the isometric axes or on lines parallel to them. Lines that are not parallel to the isometric axes, called nonisometric lines, cannot be measured. They may be drawn by plotting their measurements in an orthographic view and transferring these measurements to the corresponding isometric plane. A line drawn between the points so established will represent the desired angle (see Plate 9).

An isometric circle is drawn in much the same manner. By enclosing a circle in a square and locating the square in its proper isometric plane, the four points of contact between circle and square may be located. Using these points as guides, the circle may be roughed in freehand or laid out with a compass as indicated in Plate 9. A square in isometric drawing has two obtuse and two acute angles. From the apex of the obtuse angles A and B draw lines to the centers of the opposite sides establishing points G, H, E, and F. Two of these four lines will intersect at C, the other two at D. Place the point of the compass on C and adjust the other arm to a distance equal to CE. Draw an arc from E to H. Using the same compass reading, place the compass point at D and lay in an arc between F and G. Two segments of the isometric circle are now complete. Place the point of the compass at A and adjust its arm to a distance equal to AH. Lay in an arc from H to G. Change the point of the compass to B and draw in an arc between E and F to complete the circle.

The beginner should be aware that not all objects can be represented in isometric drawing. Since this drafting technique does not recognize the effects of foreshortening or the rules of perspective it is inevitable that some finished drawings appear distorted. This is especially true of large drawings; the larger the drawing, the more obvious the distortion becomes. Irregular shapes that do not conform to the isometric axes are difficult to draw, and, if drawn, may be so misshapen as to be of little value.

OBLIQUE DRAWING

The oblique drawing is really a combination of the principles of orthographic projection and isometric drawing. A finished drawing accomplished by this technique resembles an isometric drawing in that three faces of an object are shown in a single drawing, but one of the faces is at a right angle to the observer's line of sight as in orthographic projection.

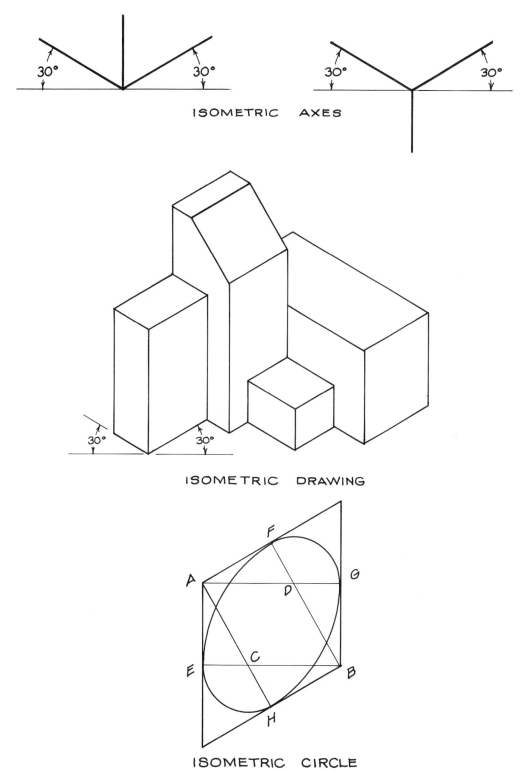

ISOMETRIC AXES

ISOMETRIC DRAWING

ISOMETRIC CIRCLE

PLATE 9

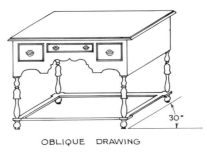

OBLIQUE   DRAWING

PLATE 10

It has been previously mentioned that irregular shapes, curves, and odd angles are difficult to draw isometrically. This problem is avoided in oblique drawing by representing the most complicated surface of an object by a direct front view. The remaining two sides of the object are drawn to the left or right of the front view at angles of 30° or 45°. When the angular lines extend upward, the object appears to be below the eye level and the top of it can be seen. When the lines are extended downward, the object appears to be above eye level and the bottom of the structure is revealed.

CABINET DRAWING

This type of pictorial drawing is not used frequently. Cabinet drawing and oblique drawing are similar in all details of construction and appearance except one; the depth or thickness measurements of a cabinet drawing are reduced by one-half or by some lesser ratio such as 2 to 3. This is done to improve the appearance of the drawing and to reduce the distortion that will occur if the depth measurement is excessive.

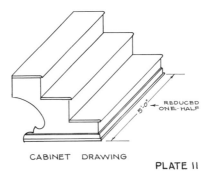

CABINET   DRAWING

PLATE 11

Two precautions should be taken when using this technique of drafting. Be sure to note the ratio of reduction on the drawing and to specify the over-all depth dimension at its true length. These precautions will prevent a carpenter from mistaking the drawing for an oblique.

6

PERSPECTIVE

In teaching classes of scenic design the author has found that a majority of
his students have had no art training of any kind; indeed, some of them have
not ever attempted to make a sketch of any kind. These students are perfectly aware of their shortcomings as designers, but as theatre workers who
may be specializing in direction, acting, or technical work, they rightly
feel the need for an understanding and an appreciation of scenic design since
it is a phase of theatre work closely related to their own. They have no
illusions as to their ability as artists, they have no intention of becoming
designers; but they do want a knowledge of the problems of scenic design,
they want to be acquainted with the requirements of a well-planned setting,
and they want to have sufficient knowledge of the subject to be able to
discuss a sketch intelligently with a designer.

A few beginners seem to have a natural aptitude for drawing and for
perspective and have little difficulty in recording their observations graphi-
cally. If asked to explain why they drew a certain line in a given direction,
they are likely to be unable to give a logical answer but will say perhaps,
"It looks right." Such students are the exceptions, however. Most of the
class is likely to find that perspective creates more problems in their drawing than anything else. Everything in their designs seems in imminent danger
of sliding off the stage into the orchestra pit or the furniture seems mysteri-
ously suspended in midair or the setting appears to be miles deep. Perspective is treated in this chapter in a manner intended to simplify it and to
show its immediate application to the problem of sketching settings for the
stage.

A sketch of a stage setting is usually drawn as if the observer were in the best seat in the theatre—in the middle of the house halfway back in the auditorium on the orchestra level. From this ideal observation point the observer looks through the frame formed by the proscenium arch and sees equal expanses of both side walls, all of the back wall, and the best view of any background vistas the designer has used. From no other seat in the house are the sight lines to a setting any better.

Although there are any number of excellent books on perspective, the subject is usually discussed in general terms and few of the books make any effort to apply perspective to the particular problems of stage use. For this reason, all of the problems in perspective in this chapter are planned from the point of view of a theatre worker; the observer in all cases is seated in some position in an auditorium. From that vantage point he is endeavoring to record the correct perspective drawing of various objects and shapes placed in given positions on a stage. These problems may be given additional meaning and interest to the students by substituting the dimensions of his own theatre and stage and by occasionally changing the form or position of the objects placed on stage.

The art of drawing three-dimensional objects on a flat plane so that they will appear to the eye in relief like the real objects is based on the acceptance of the statement that parallel lines seen receding from the eye must be represented as converging at a given point. To illustrate this statement, suppose that a three-dimensional rectangular solid about the size of a kitchen table is viewed from such an angle and position that one of its

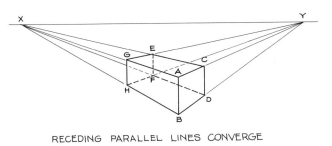

RECEDING PARALLEL LINES CONVERGE

PLATE 12

corners is nearer to us than any of the others; and suppose that the solid is below our eye level so that we can see its top (see Plate 12). It is obvious that the corner *AB* is nearer to the observer than the corners *CD* and *GH* because it appears higher than they do. As we represent this object on paper, the lines *CD* and *GH* are shorter than the line *AB* because they are farther away from the observer. It is known that the top and bottom of the solid are parallel; and yet the lines *AG* and *BH*, representing the edges of these two planes, are shown converging in the drawing. Had we drawn these lines parallel, the solid would have appeared distorted. If the lines *AG* and *BH* are extended upward, they meet at the point *X*. The points *A*, *B*, *C*, and *D* represent the end of a solid we know to be a square. If it is a square, we also know that the top and bottom of it are parallel. However, in the drawing, extensions of the lines *AC* and *BD* are not parallel, but are shown converging at the point *Y*. This example demonstrates that parallel lines seen receding from the eye of an observer are shown converging at a given point.

Sketches for stage settings made by anyone without a sound understanding of perspective are likely to contain inaccuracies that will result in impractical designs. The designs may be much too wide, too high, or too deep to be placed on any stage. Or, at the other extreme, the setting may not fill the stage, may create impossible sight lines, or may leave little space for either actors or furnishings. It therefore becomes obvious that the designer should have the ability to show in perspective the accurate size and shape of a setting, for only then can he have the full assurance that what he has drawn can be enlarged and duplicated for a stage.

The perspective sketch is intended to convey only the designer's plan and idea for a proposed setting; the technician will not actually be building from it. Nevertheless, it is essential that the sketch give a reasonably accurate picture of the setting. When the director approves a design, he has every right to expect that the constructed setting will be a three-dimensional facsmile of that design and not just a rough approximation of it.

An accurate perspective drawing demands that the following factors be known:

1 Distance of the observer from the object to be drawn
2 Level of the observer's eye above the plane upon which the object rests
3 Size and position of an object in relation to a vertical plane placed at right angles to the observer's line of sight and between him and the object

A study of the vertical section and horizontal plan of the theatre at the University of Iowa will clarify these three points (see Plates 13 and 14). The auditorium of this theatre has continental seating. Each row of seats is tiered one above the other and extends across the auditorium without interruption until meeting the side aisles. Indicated on both drawings are three observation points *A*, *B*, and *C*. An observer seated at *A* is 19'-0" from the tormentor line, at *B* 35'-6", and at *C* 65'-0". It can be seen in the vertical section that from these same observation points his eye level at *A* is 3'-0" above the stage floor, at *B* it is 6'-6", and at *C* it is 14'-6". These heights are established by drawing a sight line from each eye level parallel to the stage floor, finding the point at which these lines intersect the tormentor plane (the tormentor line), and measuring the height of these points from the stage floor. At each of these three observation points, an object placed on the stage floor will be seen from different distances and heights. As these dimensions change, so will the appearance of a perspective drawing of the object change.

The terminology used in discussing the following problems can be ex-

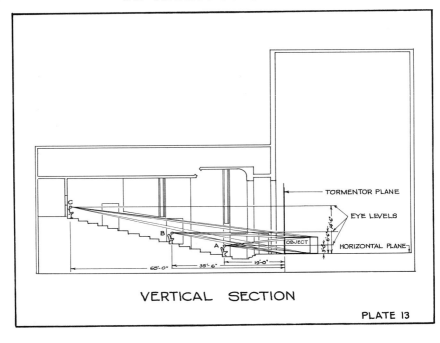

TORMENTOR PLANE

EYE LEVELS

OBJECT

HORIZONTAL PLANE

65'-0"   35'-6"   19'-0"

VERTICAL SECTION

PLATE 13

plained in part by reference to Plates 13 and 14. The positions *A*, *B*, and *C* in the auditorium mark the position of an observer whose eye level is presumed to be 4'-0" above the floor at the point where he is seated. Any one of these positions is called the "observation point." The stage floor is the "horizontal plane" where the objects to be drawn are placed. A line from *A*, *B*, or *C* at right angles to the tormentor line is the "line of direction." If a "tormentor plane," such as a transparent gauze, were suspended at the tormentor line, it would be at a right angle to the line of direction. The point at which the line of direction intersects the tormentor plane is called the "center of vision." A horizontal plane at the same height above the floor as the observer's eye level would intersect the tormentor plane and is known as the "horizon." Any lines of sight from an observer to the different corners and faces of an object on stage would intersect the tormentor plane. If all the points of intersection could be connected by lines drawn on the tormentor plane, an oversize perspective of the object would result. Since it is not practical to draw on this tormentor plane, a second vertical plane, called the "picture plane," is placed at any convenient distance nearer the observer. In the following problems the picture plane is placed at the observation point.

The diagrams used in laying out the following problems use a larger scale than that employed in drawing the entire stage and auditorium as in Plates 13 and 14. The larger scale eliminates the necessity of redrawing portions of the stage and auditorium not needed for the solution of the problem and also allows greater accuracy.

The selection of a proper scale is the first factor to consider in laying

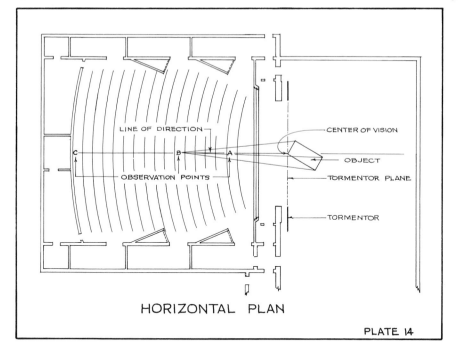

LINE OF DIRECTION

CENTER OF VISION

C B A

OBJECT

OBSERVATION POINTS

TORMENTOR PLANE

TORMENTOR

HORIZONTAL PLAN

PLATE 14

out a perspective diagram. The choice of ³⁄₁₆″, ¼″, or ³⁄₈″ scale will depend upon the size of the object and the distance of the observer from it. Care must be taken to place the diagram on the paper in such a position as to ensure that all points of the problem will fall within the limits of the paper.

Problem I

A statement of the problem illustrated in Plate 15 would appear as follows:

Scale ¼″ = 1′-0″
Observation point (OP) 28′-0″ right and 4′-0″ above
Center of vision (CV) 24′-0″ from OP
Horizon (H) 6′-0″ from OP
Object A rectangle 5′-0″ × 10′-0″ lying on the stage floor with its sides at a 45° angle to the tormentor plane (or vertical plane) and the near corner *A* in contact with the center of vision (CV)

The diagrams on which these problems are laid out consist of only four lines—one vertical and three horizontal. Each line represents some aspect of the problem and is laid out according to the directions contained in the statement. Unless otherwise specfied, all problems are arranged for a sheet of paper at least 10″ × 14″.

The first point to establish in laying out a diagram is the observation point. The problem states that the observation point (OP) is 28′-0″ right and 4′-0″ above. This simply means that OP is found by measuring on the

¼″ scale, 28′-0″ to the right of the left edge of the paper and 4′-0″ up from the bottom edge. Where these two measurements coincide is the location of OP.

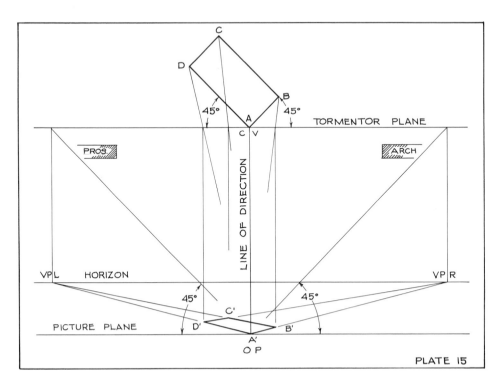

PLATE 15

From OP draw a perpendicular line to represent the line of direction (LD). From OP along LD measure off 24′-0″ and at this point draw a line at right angles to LD. This line corresponds to the tormentor plane. The point of contact between the two lines will be the center of vision (CV). The distance between OP and CV represents the distance of the observer from the nearest corner of the object, which in this problem, is in contact with CV. The picture plane is at the observation point. Draw a line at right angles to LD through OP to establish this plane. It is on this plane that the perspective of the object will be constructed. The horizon (H) is found by measuring along LD the distance specified in the problem, in this case 6′-0″ above OP. This means that the observer's eye is 6′ higher than the horizontal plane (stage floor) on which the object is resting. The object we propose to draw is a 5′ × 10′ rectangle; it is so placed on the horizontal plane that its sides form a 45° angle with the tormentor line. The near corner of the rectangle is in contact with CV.

Suppose that before we proceed with this problem, we restate it in a different way in order to illustrate its application to the theatre. Imagine that you are seated in the center of the auditorium and are looking through the proscenium arch onto the stage. Most settings are masked on the downstage sides by tormentors (vertical masking pieces placed on either side of the stage, parallel with the proscenium arch, but two or more feet upstage of it). Your seat in the auditorium is 24′ from an extension of the tormentor line. At this distance from the stage your eye level is 6′ above the stage floor. A small flat is lying in the center of the stage with one corner touching this extension of the tormentor line and with its sides forming a 45° angle with it. Under these conditions you propose to make a perspective drawing of the flat.

After laying out the diagram, the first step in solving any perspective problem is establishing the vanishing points for all receding lines. A vanishing point is that point on the horizon at which all lines parallel to each other converge. All the lines in a group of parallel lines, regardless of their position in relation to the object being drawn, have the same vanishing point; they are known as a system of lines. Consult Plate 15 for a moment. Two systems of lines are apparent from the shape of the object. Since it is rectangular in form, the lines *AD* and *BC* are parallel; and they form one system. The lines *AB* and *DC* are also parallel, and they form the second system. Each system has its own vanishing point—one to the left and one to the right. To find the vanishing point for the lines *AB* and *DC* draw a line parallel to them from OP until it intersects the tormentor plane. From the point of intersection drop a line parallel to LD until it meets the horizon. This establishes the right vanishing point (VPR). The same procedure is followed to find the vanishing point for the lines *AD* and *BC*. The line from OP would run to the left of LD rather than to the right. From the point of intersection with the tormentor plane drop a line to the horizon to establish the left vanishing point (VPL).

Any part of an object that is in contact with the tormentor plane is unaffected by perspective and may be dropped parallel to LD to the picture plane. Corner *A* is the only point touching the tormentor plane; and it may be located on the picture plane by projecting its position down parallel to LD. The new point *A′* happens to coincide with OP in this problem. From *A′* draw light guide lines to VPL and VPR. Somewhere along these lines will fall the perspective of lines *AD* and *AB*.

The perspective of the line *AB* is found as follows. Draw a light sight line from OP to corner *B* of the rectangle. From the point at which the sight line intersects the tormentor plane, drop a line parallel to LD until it intersects the guide line *A′* VPR. The point of intersection between the two lines establishes *B′*. *A′B′* is the true perspective of the line *AB*. The same procedure is followed in finding *A′D′*, but note that this line is controlled by VPL, not VPR. We now have two sides of the rectangle drawn in perspective represented by the lines *A′D′* and *A′B′*.

We know from looking at the object in diagram that *DC* is parallel to *AB*. Therefore, both lines will have the same vanishing point—VPR. The same is true for the lines *AD* and *BC*, except that the vanishing point is

VPL. Since we have already established *A'D'* and *A'B'*, the perspective can
be completed by drawing lines from *D'* to VPR, and from *B'* to VPL. Point
C' falls at the point at which these two lines intersect. The accuracy of
point *C'* may be checked by drawing a sight line from OP to *C*; from the
point at which this line intersects the tormentor plane drop a line parallel
to LD to meet either *D'*VPR or *B'*VPL. The point *C'* will be in the same
position if found by either method. The completed figure *A'B'C'D'* is an
accurate perspective drawing of the object *ABCD*.

Problem II

The closer the horizon (eye level) is to the horizontal plane (stage floor),
the less an observer will see of the true shape of the object. Problem II illustrates this statement (see Plate 16).

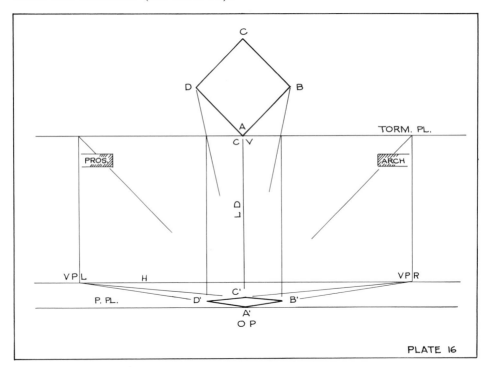

Scale ¼″ = 1′-0″
OP 28′-0″ right and 6′-0″ above
CV 20′-0″ from OP
H 3′-0″ from OP
Picture plane at OP
Object An 8′-0″ square resting on the stage floor with its sides at a 45°
    angle to the tormentor plane and the near corner *A* in contact with CV

To derive any benefit from this study in perspective, the student designer must do more than just look at the completed drawings in this book. He must actually lay out the diagram for each problem, solve it by applying the procedural steps outlined in problem I, and then compare his findings with those in the illustration which accompanies each problem. Only in such a manner can he train his eye and mind to see each logical step. Finding the solutions for the first few problems may be troublesome and time consuming, but with each problem solved there comes added understanding, until each step becomes almost mechanical.

Problem III

In the preceding problems the near corner of the object coincides with the center of vision, a most unlikely spot for a designer to place anything on stage. Problem III illustrates the principle of drawing in perspective an object that may be placed either to the left or right of the center of vision (see Plate 17).

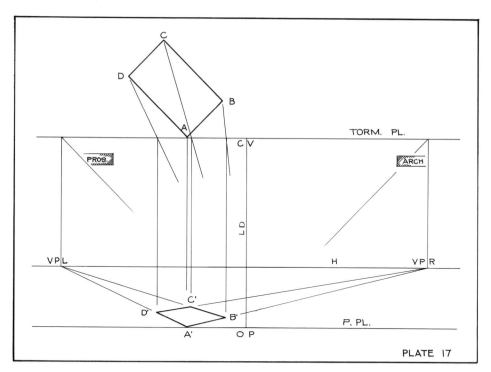

PLATE 17

Scale ¼″ = 1′-0″
OP 28′-0″ right and 4′-0″ above
CV 22′-0″ from OP
H 7′-0″ from OP
Picture plane at OP
Object A rectangle 6′-0″ × 10′-0″ with its sides at a 45° angle to the

tormentor plane. The near corner *A* is 7′-0″ to the left of CV and in contact with the tormentor plane.

Since point *A* is in contact with the tormentor plane, it may be dropped directly to the picture plane. Connect *A′* with VPL and VPR. Draw all sight lines from OP to corners *B*, *C*, and *D* of the object. From the points at which these lines intersect the tormentor plane drop a line parallel to LD to the guide lines *A′*VPL or *A′*VPR to find *B′*, *C′*, and *D′*. Note, of course, that *D′* and *C′* are located by intersections on the line to VPL and *B′* by an intersection on the line to VPR.

Problem IV

Finding the perspective of an object which has height, as well as width and length, advances one step further than the solutions for the preceding problems (see Plate 18).

Scale   ¼″ = 1′-0″
OP   41′-0″ right and 5′-0″ above
CV   23′-0″ from OP
H   8′-0″ from OP
Picture plane   at OP
Object   A platform 8′-0″ square by 3′-6″ high is placed on stage with its sides forming 30° and 60° angles to the tormentor plane. Corner *A* of the platform is 12′-0″ to the left of CV and is in contact with the tormentor plane.

We know that any point of an object in contact with the tormentor plane is unaffected by perspective, so we can drop corner *A* directly to the picture plane to find *A′*. Since *A* is not affected by perspective it is possible to measure its true height by erecting a vertical line from *A′*. Scale off its height of 3′-6″ to find *A″* which will represent the top front corner of the platform. Draw guide lines from both *A′* and *A″* to VPL and VPR. By use of the lower guide lines the perspective of the bottom of the platform can be found. The upper guide lines are used in establishing the perspective of the platform top.

Problem V

Many student designers have trouble drawing furniture so that it appears to be resting solidly on the floor and so that it bears some relationship to a wall of the room. Most furniture can be drawn easily by fitting it into an imaginary crate that is rectangular or square in shape. If the student can draw the perspective of such shapes (as in problem IV) and can combine it with the principle demonstrated in problem V he will have little trouble in making the furniture appear to be resting solidly on the floor in the desired

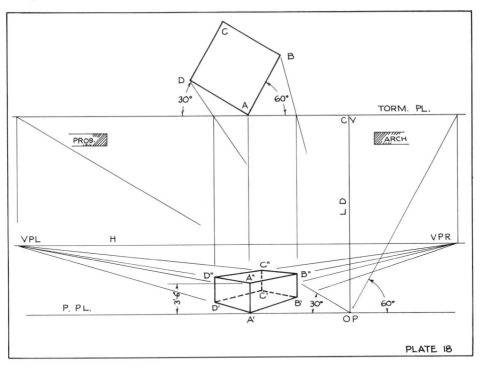

PLATE 18

position within the set. Problem V illustrates the procedure for drawing the perspective of an object that is placed beyond the tormentor plane (see Plate 19).

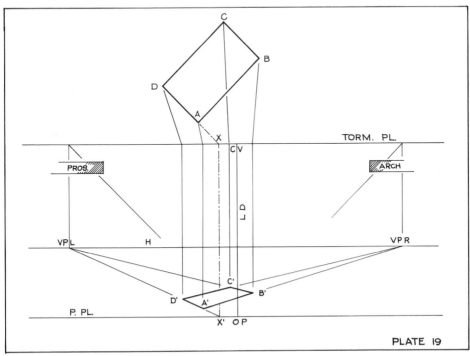

PLATE 19

Scale   ¼″ = 1′-0″
OP   28′-0″ right and 4′-0″ above
CV   20′-0″ from OP
H   8′-0″ from OP
Picture plane   at OP
Object   A small flat, 6′-0″ × 10′-6″, lying on the stage floor with its sides
    at a 45° angle to the tormentor plane. The near corner *A* is 4′-6″ left of
    CV and 2′-6″ upstage of it.

Extend the side of the flat *DA* until it meets the tormentor plane at *X*.
Draw a line from *X* to the picture plane parallel to LD to find *X′*. Draw a
guide line from *X′* to VPL. The perspective of *AD* will be found somewhere
along the line *X′*VPL. Draw sight lines from OP to *A* and *D*, and at their
intersection with the tormentor plane drop them down in the usual manner
to find *A′* and *D′* on the guide line *X′*VPL. It is possible to find the perspective of the flat by extending any one of its sides to the tormentor plane and
proceeding as outlined. The sides *AB* and *DC* will, of course, be controlled
by VPR rather than VPL.

Problem VI

The procedure for finding the vanishing points of objects whose sides are
parallel with the line of direction is exactly the same as that followed in
all preceding problems.

Scale   ¼″ = 1′-0″
OP   28′-0″ right and 3′-6″ above
CV   20′-0″ from OP
H   6′-0″ above OP
Picture plane   at OP
Object   A ceiling piece 10′-0″ × 14′-0″, lying on the stage floor with its
    longer sides parallel to the tormentor plane, but with the nearer of the
    two sides 2′-0″ beyond the tormentor plane. The vertical plane (V.Pl.),
    or tormentor plane, has been placed in line with the outer face of the
    proscenium arch in this problem. The dimensions of the proscenium arch
    are 32′-0″ wide by 16′-0″ high with walls 1′-0″ thick. In this problem we
    propose to find the perspective of both the proscenium and the ceiling
    piece.

Draw a line from OP parallel to the sides of the object until it intersects
the tormentor plane. From there drop a line, parallel to LD until it meets H.
This establishes the central vanishing point (VPC).

Find the perspective of the proscenium arch first. We know that the
on-stage corners of the proscenium arch are in contact with the tormentor
plane and so may be dropped directly to the picture plane to establish *E′*

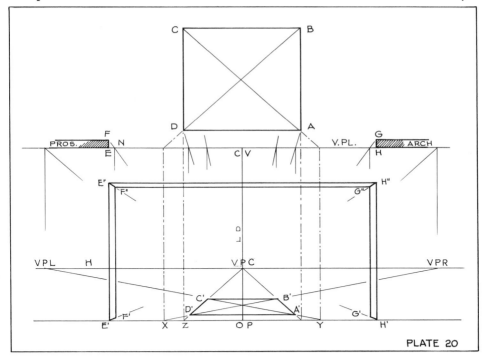

PLATE 20

and *H'*. Since these two points are unaffected by perspective, the height of 16'-0" can be measured off to find *E"* and *H"*. Connect *E"* and *H"* by a horizontal line that will represent the top of the proscenium arch. This establishes the perspective of the outer face of the proscenium arch as represented by the lines *E'E"*, *E"H"*, and *H"H'*. We know by looking at the diagram that the thickness lines of the arch at its junction with the stage floor and at its top are parallel to LD; therefore, all lines representing the depth of the arch would be governed by the same vanishing point—VPC.

The perspective of the 1'-0" depth of the arch is found by drawing a guide line from any one of the four established corners of the arch *E'*, *E"*, *H"*, or *H'* to VPC and locating on this line the depth measurement. For example, draw a guide line to VPC from *E'*. A sight line from OP to *F* crosses the tormentor plane at *N*. Drop a line from *N* to intersect the guide line *E'*VPC. This establishes the depth of 1'-0", shown as *F'*. Once the depth measurement has been found, it can be carried around parallel to the outer face of the arch to find the perspective of its upstage edges.

The sides of the ceiling piece *CD* and *BA* are parallel to the thickness of the proscenium wall. These form a system of lines and have the same vanishing point—VPC. Since the ceiling lies 2'-0" upstage of the tormentor plane, the perspective of it can be found by the same method used in problem V. Extend the side *CD* to the tormentor plane and project it from the point of intersection down to the picture plane at Z. A guide line from Z to VPC is then drawn. From the points at which sight lines from OP to *C* and *D* cross the tormentor plane drop lines to meet the guide line Z-VPC. This establishes points *C′* and *D′*.

The perspective for the ceiling may be found by another method. Using the diagonals of the ceiling *DB* and *AC* find the vanishing points for these two lines as in previous problems. Extend the diagonals until they meet the tormentor plane, and from these points drop lines straight down to the picture plane to establish *X* and *Y*. Draw guide lines from *X* to VPR and from *Y* to VPL. Draw sight lines from OP to the corners of the ceiling *C*, *B*, *D*, and *A*. From the points at which these sight lines intersect the tormentor plane, project lines down to the two lines just drawn to find *C′*, *B′*, *D′* and *A′*. Connect these four points for a perspective drawing of the ceiling.

Problem VII

All the procedures used in the preceding problems are used to find the perspective of a complete setting and proscenium arch (see Plate 21).

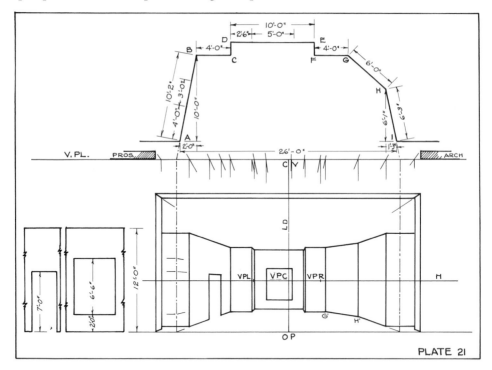

PLATE 21

Scale   ¼″ = 1′-0″
OP   33′-0″ right and 3′-0″ above
CV   20′-0″ from OP
H   6′-0″ above OP
Picture plane   at OP
Object   A simple box setting is represented by its ground plan. Vertical

dimensions of the walls, door, and window are shown on the accompanying elevations. The tormentor plane has been moved to place it in line with the outer face of the proscenium arch. The proscenium arch is 32'-0" wide, 16'-0" high, and 1'-0" thick. Notice that the side walls of the setting have been opened out, or raked, to provide better sight lines from the extreme side seats of the auditorium.

It is evident from a study of the ground plan that four vanishing points are required for this problem: one for each of the side walls, one for those lines parallel with LD, and a fourth for that section of the wall stage left marked *GH*. Find the vanishing points for the side walls first by applying the principle illustrated in problem IV. Lines parallel to LD, i.e., the thickness of the proscenium arch and the lines *CD* and *EF* of the window alcove, will be governed by a central vanishing point as in problem VI. The perspective of the angular wall *GH* may be found in one of two ways. Either find a separate vanishing point for it and proceed as usual; or, locate point *G'* on the perspective of the back wall and *H'* on the stage left wall. A line between these two points will establish its perspective without actually using a vanishing point.

Problem VIII

The perspective for circular or curved lines can be found by enclosing them within a geometric form and by plotting the points of contact between the graph lines and the contour lines (see Plate 22).

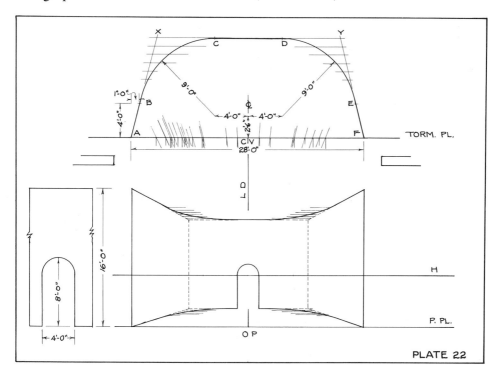

PLATE 22

Scale ¼″ = 1′-0″
OP 28′-0″ right and 4′-0″ above
CV 22′-0″ from OP
H 6′-0″ above OP
Picture plane at OP
Object The shape of a small set with curved walls is described by the dimensions shown on the accompanying ground plan. The walls are 16′-0″ high. The downstage ends of the walls are in contact with the tormentors.

Find the vanishing points for the straight sections of the walls, *AB* and *EF* by the usual method. Extend the walls *AB* and *EF* until they are as deep as the center section of the set. A line passing through the straight section of the back wall (*CD*) and extended parallel to the tormentor plane will intersect the side wall extensions at *X* and *Y*. This determines the depth of the set. Draw a series of graph lines parallel to the tormentor plane to intersect the extension lines and the curve of the side walls. There may be any number of these graph lines spaced at any desired distance from each other. The more graph lines there are, the more points of reference there will be; hence the resultant perspective will be more accurate. Establish in perspective the points of intersection between the graph and contour lines. Using a French curve (a curved piece of celluloid or plastic, often in the form of a scroll, used as an aid in drawing noncircular curves) lay a continuous line passing through these points for a perspective drawing of the curved walls.

Problem IX

This problem illustrates two principles—the effect in perspective of an object placed at an extreme distance to one side of CV and the diminishing effect on the horizontal planes of the stair treads when the horizon is at some point between the top and bottom of the stairway (see Plate 23).

Scale ¼″ = 1′-0″
OP 28′-0″ right and 3′-0″ above
CV 22′-0″ from OP
H 5′-0″ above OP
Picture plane at OP
Object An angular staircase fitted against two walls of a setting—the stage right wall and a section of the rear wall. The stage right wall is in contact with the tormentor plane 22′-0″ to the left of CV. The stairway is 3′-0″ wide with 1′-0″ treads and 6″ risers. Additional dimensions for laying out the diagram are shown on the plan and elevations.

A study of the plan shows that three vanishing points could be used in solving this problem. One would be for those lines parallel to AC, another for those parallel to *BE*, and a third for that system of lines represented by

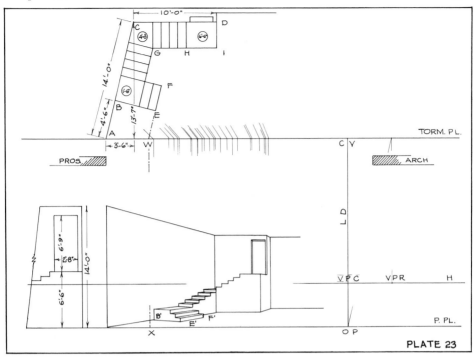

PLATE 23

ID. However, the vanishing point for *BE* would be inconvenient to use since it would fall at some point beyond the limit of the paper. In this case, the perspective can be found without the left vanishing point. Extend a plane of the stairway, such as *EF*, to the tormentor plane at *W*, and then project it parallel to LD until it meets the picture plane (at *X*). The perspective of line *EF* can be found on a guide line from *X* to the VPR. A line from *E′* to *B′* will be the perspective of line *EB*. The vertical height of the steps adjacent to the back wall can be found by extending the plane of each step to the tormentor plane and picture plane and measuring its height along this line.

Problem X

Problem X provides the student with an opportunity to compare the accuracy of his reconstructed perspective drawing with a photograph of the setting taken with the camera placed at the observation point (see Plates 24–27). If circumstances will permit it, additional interest can be given to this last problem by reconstructing the perspective of whatever setting happens to be on stage at the moment. The accuracy of the perspective can be checked against the setting on stage by comparing the two from the same observation point.

Scale ⅜″ = 1′-0″
OP 24′-6″ right and 8′-6″ above
CV 36′-0″ from OP

H 7'-0" from OP

Picture plane at OP

Object The ground plan for the Act I bar and family room setting used for a production of Eugene O'Neill's *Anna Christie*. All additional measurements needed for laying out the diagram are shown on the ground plan or on the elevation (Plates 24 and 26).

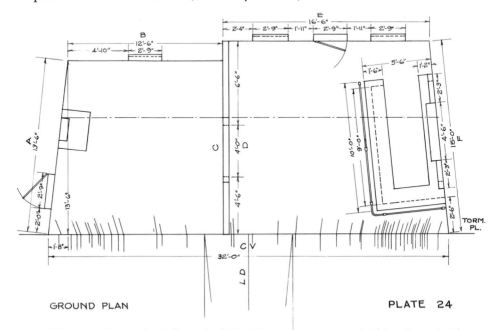

GROUND PLAN   PLATE 24

Mount a sheet of 1'-6" × 2'-0" detail paper on your drafting board. Turn the drafting board to place the 2'-0" length of the paper in a vertical position; in this problem a larger scale and a greater distance between OP and the tormentor plane require the larger paper.

Two new features are of special interest in this problem. One is the

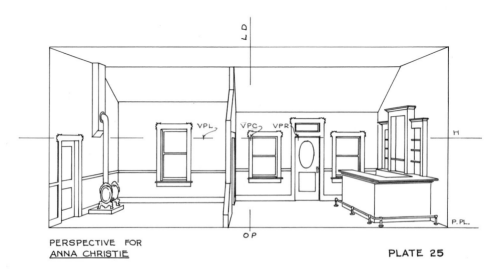

PERSPECTIVE FOR
ANNA CHRISTIE   PLATE 25

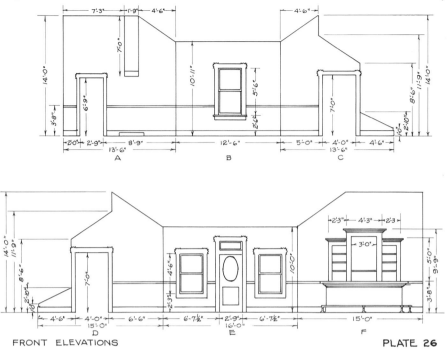

FRONT ELEVATIONS   PLATE 26

effect of foreshortening apparent on the partition that separates the two rooms of the setting; and the other is the slanting ceiling adjacent to the back wall. Because of foreshortening, little of the true shape of the partition can be shown since the downstage end of it is almost in line with OP. The perspective of the slanting ceiling in the bar can be drawn by establishing two points—the height of the back wall at its junction with the stage left wall and that point on the stage left wall where the slanting ceiling

PLATE 27 *Anna Christie*, produced at the University Theatre, State University of Iowa, directed by Paul Davee, designed by A. S. Gillette

meets the horizontal ceiling. A line drawn between these two points will represent the junction between the slanting ceiling and the side wall. Although the family room is 1'-6" less in depth than the bar, the same procedure can be followed to find the perspective of the slanting ceiling in that part of the setting.

In summing up the work on perspective one point should be made perfectly clear. It is not the intention of the author to suggest that all sketches for the stage should be drawn by utilizing the mechanical procedures outlined in this chapter. This practice would be neither feasible nor desirable. It is not feasible because it requires too much time and because it demands that all dimensions be known at a point in the designer's procedure when he is just attempting to establish them. It is not desirable because sketches drawn in this manner are too mechanical in appearance and because they lose whatever individualistic style the artist has to characterize his drawing. These problems are presented here to help the beginner understand the principles of perspective as they are applied to the special problems of designing for the stage. He may use perspective as a tool and as a method of checking his work, but it should not dominate his style of rendering nor curtail his imagination.

7

THE WATER COLOR
SKETCH

Just how does the designer commit his ideas to paper? As we have said before, no two designers work in exactly the same way; each finds a method which is satisfactory for him but which differs from another's method. The important thing is that the designer places his ideas on paper in a legible fashion so that others can clearly see his intentions.

After all preliminary work has been completed, most designers begin work on a play, even a simple one requiring only one setting, by placing their first ideas on paper in a series of small pencil drawings called thumbnail sketches. These preliminary sketches are usually quite rough and often almost meaningless to anyone but the designer. They are small, not scaled, and quickly done. They are the designer's first efforts to coordinate the findings of his research with the requirements of the play and of the director. He is literally feeling his way at this point as he tries out first one scheme and then another. Perhaps he has found an especially attractive fireplace that he would like to use. If he attempts to place it in the back wall where it would show off to best advantage, it is in a poor position for the extensive stage business the director wants his actors to perform around it. So a second thumbnail sketch has the fireplace downstage right, in a much better position for the stage business, but in this new position it can't be seen as well. Changing the angle of the side wall brings the fireplace into better view and still keeps it in a position where it can be used to good advantage by the director. A third sketch is done to show this new idea. Each major

The setting as suggested in script. Much used kitchen fireplace in awkward position for actors. Two-level floor makes square dancing impossible.

Kitchen fireplace in better position, but kitchen area too small and partition reduces dancing space.

Better placement of kitchen fireplace makes it easy for actors to "open up." Angle of back wall excessive, resulting in poor sight lines stage left.

THUMBNAIL SKETCHES FOR
CHANCELLOR'S PARTY

PLATE 28

change in the setting will probably require a new sketch until the designer is finally satisfied with an arrangement of architectural features and a furniture layout.

CHANCELLOR'S PARTY   PLATE 29

Asking "Which comes first, the ground plan or the sketch?" is like asking about chickens and eggs. Each designer must find his own answer to this question. Some begin their work with rough ground plans. They may even lay out an arrangement of the whole house or apartment from which their setting is to be selected. By following such a painstaking procedure, the designer can see if the plan of his setting is logical when considered in relation to the rest of the house. Certainly this approach makes it easier to detect such architectural errors as windows shown on each side of a doorway that supposedly opens into an adjacent room or a stairway that would have to extend outside the walls of a house in order to reach the second story. Other designers, instead of beginning with ground plans, visualize a setting by seeing it in perspective first; and then they develop a ground plan to fit the sketch. Whichever scheme seems easier is correct.

On viewing his collection of thumbnail sketches, the designer may find something he likes in each of them, but no single sketch which incorporates all his good ideas. In one sketch is a stairway treatment he likes, in another the furniture arrangement catches his fancy, in the third the wall treatment is particularly successful, and in the fourth the location of the main entrance works well. He may select one or two features from each of his sketches and then combine them in a final thumbnail sketch. The final sketch is more carefully drawn, and in it he makes the adjustments and alterations necessary for good composition. At this point the designer is ready to transfer his design from thumbnail sketch to the final water color rendering.

The material in this chapter concerns itself with some of the problems involved in transparent water color rendering. Of course, transparent water colors are not the only acceptable way to color stage designs. The designer is free to select any medium he likes, as long as it provides the color he wants and is permanent enough to withstand the rigors of production conferences. Excellent stage designs have been made with washes of colored ink, charcoal and ink washes, opaque water color, colored pencils, indelible pencils, and pastels. Many of these mediums combine readily with transparent water colors, and a combination may produce an effect difficult to obtain when using any one of them alone. Since water color rendering is one of the fastest methods of coloring a design, and since it provides a color that will not rub off or smear, it is favored by most scene designers.

Before starting work on the color rendering, it is well to consult with the director to get his last-minute reactions to and suggestions about the final thumbnail sketch. Remember that while the designer has been doing research and preliminary sketches, the director also has been thinking about the play and has started planning stage business and movement for his actors and preliminary blocking. What he wanted in his setting four days ago may have changed and he may now prefer to see a little different arrangement. It is certainly easier to make such changes in a sketch before the design has been rendered in color. The precaution of a conference at this stage helps assure that the color sketch will have all features of the setting arranged in their proper places, and it may eliminate the need for doing a second color rendering in order to include the changes.

Mount the water color paper or illustration board on the drafting board so that both T square and triangle can be used in laying out the sketch, place the final thumbnail sketch where you can see it easily, and you are ready to transfer your design to its final form. The first step in this final drawing is selecting the proper scale and measuring off a rectangular frame that will represent the actual size of your proscenium opening. Give some thought to the proper spacing of the proscenium opening on the drawing paper; it should be centered from the sides but preferably have more border at the bottom than at the top. The wider border at the bottom leaves room for title, date, and your name. Carefully measuring and drawing a frame that represents the actual size of the proscenium arch is most important because this frame can then serve as a reference point for the accuracy and scale of anything that is drawn in back of it. Suppose that the proscenium opening is 34′ wide and has a teaser setting of 14′. On the ½″ scale this is represented by a rectangle 17″ × 7″. Since the proscenium frame is to scale, it is possible to measure the height of the horizon line and to establish on it the approximate location of those vanishing points that will be needed in plotting the layout of the setting. As a further aid to accuracy of scale, many designers measure off the height of a 6′ actor at one side of the proscenium and some even draw in a stick figure to represent him. With this visual reminder constantly at hand, it isn't likely that a doorway will be drawn much too large or too small for the actor's use or that furniture will be drawn too far out of proportion to his size.

The final thumbnail sketch is used as a guide in transferring the design to the larger scale required for the colored sketch. First, the floor line of the setting should be blocked in. This allows one to visualize the position and shape of the setting with respect to the proscenium arch and to do so with the fewest possible lines. If the floor lines seem satisfactory, the vertical wall sections and the ceiling line can then be blocked in.

It is most important during this "blocking-in period" to draw very lightly and to use a hard pencil, nothing softer than a 3H. It may be necessary to redraw portions of the sketch several times before the desired effect is obtained. Heavy pencil lines require vigorous erasing which may roughen the surface of the drawing paper so that that part of the paper will receive water color paint differently from the rest of the surface. It is equally important that the drawing be kept as free as possible from pencil shading and graphite glaze. Both have a tendency to make the surface of the drawing paper seem oily and it then becomes difficult to paint over this surface. Graphite glaze is a film of pencil lead that is smeared over a drawing by the underside of the T square and triangles or by the designer's hands, and it is caused by using a pencil that is too soft.

When the shape of the room has been clearly defined by its walls, it becomes comparatively easy to locate and sketch in the doors, windows, and special features such as a fireplace or stairway. The introduction of these elements may necessitate some readjustment of the wall areas, and this is still another reason for drawing lightly at this time. With all the physical features of the setting drawn, the furniture arrangement can be blocked in. Remember that the arrangement of the furniture should bear some relationship to the form of the room and, at the same time, it should provide the director with a plan that allows him the greatest possible variety for planning the movement and groupings for his actors.

The furniture may be drawn with as much detail as desired once its position has been established. In some cases it will be necessary to erase the light lines of the setting, e.g., where the furniture covers a section of wall or part of a doorway or step unit. More attention can now be paid to completing the details of the setting, drawing in a baseboard, paneling, a chair rail, and similar features not covered by the furniture. Usually, the last items to be drawn in a sketch are the window curtains, pictures, small props, electrical fixtures, and wall hangings. In most cases it is advisable to clean fingerprints, smudges, and unnecessary lines off the finished pencil sketch before attempting to paint it. A soft, pliable, pink eraser that has been sharpened to a chisel edge can be used for this purpose, but care must be exercised not to damage the surface of the illustration board by too energetic a scrubbing.

Materials for Rendering in Transparent Water Color

The materials needed for rendering in transparent water color are not expensive and can usually be obtained in any well-stocked art dealer's shop or bookstore. These supplies consist of paper or illustration boards, brushes, transparent water color pigments, a mixing palette, and a water container.

WATER COLOR PAPER OR ILLUSTRATION BOARD

The colored sketch may be drawn on any good quality water color paper or illustration board. If water color paper is used, it must be properly mounted on the drawing board to prevent its curling or buckling when the water color pigments are applied. It would be well to inquire from the dealer how a particular paper should be mounted, since there are so many different types of paper available. Select a paper that does not have too rough a surface texture. Fine details, such as knickknacks on the fireplace mantel, or the smaller pieces of furniture are difficult to draw and paint unless the paper has a fairly smooth surface. Whatever water color paper is selected, it is advisable to protect the finished sketch by mounting it behind a frame made of heavy cardboard. Many designers prefer to use illustration board instead of the lighter weight water color paper. A sheet of illustration board 15″ × 20″ is a little more expensive than a single sheet of water color paper, but it has the advantages of not curling or buckling when water color is applied and it requires no special mounting frame.

PAINT BRUSHES

Good quality brushes have red sable bristles which will retain a point and have adequate spine to spring back into shape even when wet. Economize, if necessary, on anything else in the designer's supplies, but do not economize on the price paid for brushes. Cheap brushes are almost impossible to use. They will not retain a point. The bristles splay out until they resemble the hair-do of a beatnik. Because of an inadequate spine they will not straighten out when freshly wet, but will retain the same shape they had when last used.

At least two sizes of brushes are required—a number 5, used principally for detail work, and a number 7, used for background washes. Other size brushes, both larger and smaller, are convenient to use for special effects, but satisfactory work can be done with the two sizes mentioned.

TRANSPARENT WATER COLOR PIGMENTS

There are two kinds of water color paint—transparent and opaque. Transparent paint, when properly mixed with water, creates a thin wash that is literally transparent. It is possible to see through one wash to another or to see the outline of a drawing beneath it. Opaque paints, sometimes called show card colors, tempera, or gouache, are rarely used in rendering stage designs.

Transparent water colors come in two forms—moist and dry. The moist pigment is usually sold in tubes and is easier to use since large quantities of it can be mixed in very little time. When moist water colors are used, care must be taken to recap the tube immediately or the pigment will dry out and harden. The inside of the cap should be kept free of pigment to avoid the cap's sticking to the tube. If too much pressure is used in trying to unscrew the cap, the lead foil tube is likely to split open. Stuck caps can be loosened by holding the tube under hot running water or by heating the cap with a match. Dry pigments are sold in cakes or pans and are usually kept in a metal box with a hinged top which can be used as a mixing palette. Some of the dry pigments are very hard, and it requires much time to soften them up enough to use. It is also difficult to keep the pans of dry color clean, since dabs and smears of other pigments are frequently mixed with them.

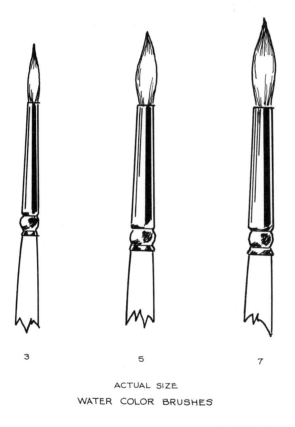

3   5   7

ACTUAL SIZE
WATER COLOR BRUSHES

PLATE 30

The choice between moist and dry pigment is up to the individual; good work can be done with either. The author would probably choose moist paints, and if asked to recommend a brand, would probably name the Scholastic Water Colors manufactured by Windsor and Newton, Ltd., of London, England. These colors are brilliant in hue, fade little, and are easily procured. While the color chart of the company lists forty-two

different hues available in tube colors, the beginner needs only a dozen or
so hues. A minimum list of colors should include the following:

> Cadmium yellow (brilliant yellow)
> Vermilion, middle tint (reddish orange)
> Yellow ochre (yellowish tan)
> Raw sienna (golden tan)
> Alizarin crimson (saturated red)
> Burnt sienna (brick red)
> Raw umber (earthy brown)
> Viridian tint (blue-green)
> Hooker's green (saturated green)
> Cobalt blue (light blue)
> Ultramarine blue (saturated blue)
> Van Dyke brown (dark brown)
> Ivory black (black)

MIXING PALETTE

A color slant, or mixing palette, is essential for mixing transparent
water colors. Mixing palettes are trays, usually made of china or enamel-
lined metal, and they are available in many different sizes and shapes. If
money is no object, one may even purchase disposable plastic palettes and

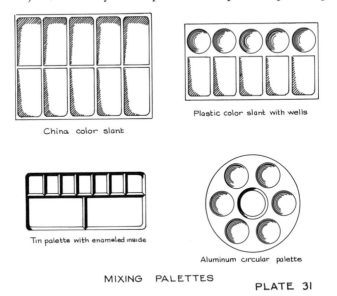

China color slant

Plastic color slant with wells

Tin palette with enameled inside

Aluminum circular palette

MIXING PALETTES

PLATE 31

use a fresh one each time. Each tray has a series of slanting indentures or
circular wells large enough to hold a quantity of mixed paint. A designer
will need a color slant with enough indentures to handle at least eight or
ten separate washes. The mixing surface must be pure white so that the
exact hue of color being mixed can be judged. The color slant should be
washed immediately after each use. At that time it can be cleaned easily

by holding it under running water for a few moments, but if the pigment is allowed to dry in little piles on the face of a slant, much more time will be needed to clean it.

WATER CONTAINERS

Almost any sort of water container may be used as long as it is not too small. A small glass of water can be discolored by washing a single brush of paint in it; if this discolored water is used for mixing a new wash of paint, the new paint will then be slightly discolored. It is advisable to use two containers, one with fresh water for mixing the paint and one for washing soiled brushes. Sauce bowls about 6″ or 8″ in diameter are ideal.

Experiments and Practice in Water Color Techniques

Before returning to the discussion of rendering a water color sketch, the author wants to urge the beginning student to experiment with his brushes and colors. As a beginning, try mixing a small quantity of wash. Squeeze a little of the pigment (about ³⁄₁₆″ or ¼″) from a tube onto the upper face of an indenture of the color slant. Moisten a brush with water and add it, a little at a time, to the pigment, mixing the two together with the brush. The resultant wash will gather at the bottom of the indenture and be ready for use. The more water added, the lighter in brilliance the wash becomes.

See how much area can be covered with a given amount of wash. Rendering a sketch involves covering different areas with washes of varying hues, and since it is difficult to mix two washes that are identical in hue and brilliance, it is desirable to mix an adequate supply of a wash before starting to paint.

Now try mixing two different colors together, for instance, blue and yellow. How many different hues of green can be obtained? What happens if you paint over a dried clear yellow wash with a clear blue wash? Is the resulting green different from the green obtained by mixing directly on the color slant? Notice what occurs when a wash is applied to the paper, allowed to dry, and then is repainted with the same wash. Although no additional pigment is added to the wash on the color slant, the wash on the paper now appears much darker. Since water colors are transparent, it is possible to add one wash on top of another in a series of applications to darken a color without changing its hue.

Mix together two colors that you would not ordinarily think of combining, for example, ultramarine blue and raw umber or vermilion and cobalt blue. What is the resultant hue? The possibilities of color mixture are almost unlimited, and the more one experiments with it, the more he appreciates its wide range. A delightful characteristic of water color sketching is that it's difficult not to learn something new about it each time colors are mixed or a brush is applied to paper.

Most renderings of set designs are painted by either a flat or graded wash or by a combination of the two types. The flat wash is basic and must be mastered to achieve a uniform application of pigment over a given area. The secret of laying a smooth wash is in establishing and maintaining an elongated puddle of pigment at the bottom of each horizontal brush stroke and in moving this puddle progressively from top to bottom of a given area. Any excess paint remaining in the puddle when the lower limit of a wash is reached can be blotted up with a brush that has been wiped by a clean cloth. A flat wash is not difficult to do provided the following suggestions are kept in mind: keep the drawing board tipped toward you at a slight angle so the wash will gather at the bottom of each brush stroke; use a large brush well charged with paint; have an adequate supply of wash in the mixing palette before starting; and work easily and rapidly.

Sunset effects, shadows in the corners of a room, the weathered appearance of an old barn, or the dirty look of an unkempt cellar are gained by using variations of a graded wash. This may be a wash that progresses from dark to light, from light to dark, or from one color to another. The graded wash is laid in much the same manner as a flat wash; its success depends principally on how well the elongated puddle has been maintained and moved progressively over the wash area. If the wash is to be graded from dark to light, proceed as follows: after the puddle has been established, recharge the brush with wash, dip it lightly into clear water, and then apply the wash again to the paper. Repeat this procedure with each recharging of the brush, gradually increasing the amount of clear water added at each recharging. Another method for achieving the same results is to add water gradually to the reserve wash supply. This method requires slightly more time, but the results are easier to control. The same technique is used in reverse for a wash that is to be graded from light to dark or from one color to another.

No amount of reading about laying a smooth graded wash will benefit a student as much as actually practicing the process. He will learn from experience just how much water must be added to a wash to change its brilliance, and he will also learn to work easily but rapidly. While practicing washes of different kinds, it is an excellent idea to confine them to boundaries of various shapes. Enclose a circle within a square, and cover each with separate washes. See how closely the washes can be brought to the boundary lines without overlapping. What happens if the first wash is still damp when the second is applied? Experiment!

The Pencil Sketch Before Coloring

The size of the final water color sketch is determined by two factors—the size of the stage and the scale to be used. Probably more sketches are made on the ½″ = 1′-0″ scale than any other. Since the average proscenium opening is about 32' wide, the use of this scale results in a sketch that is 16" wide and 6"-8" high, depending on the height at which the teaser is set. If a smaller scale is used, the sketch is proportionally smaller, and it becomes increasingly difficult to show all of the necessary details. An additional disadvantage of the small sketch is the difficulty of rendering it clearly in color. Sketches made on a scale larger than $\frac{1}{2}$" = 1'-0" require more time to render and may be too large to handle and carry around conveniently.

Coloring the Sketch

The number of mistakes made in coloring a sketch can be reduced if the color scheme for the design is carefully planned in advance. The designer usually has particular colors in mind for walls, window drapes, and so on, but until he is ready to color his sketch, he has not had the opportunity to test these colors on paper or to see the effect they have on each other. Before touching the sketch with a brush it is a wise precaution to test the color scheme in all its detail on a separate sheet of illustration board. Adjustments in hue, brilliance, and degree of neutralization can be made without the risk of ruining the penciled sketch by applying to it a poorly selected color. Remember that once a water color wash has been applied to a sketch, there is no successful way to remove it.

When the color scheme has been established to the designer's satisfaction, a second precautionary measure should be taken. Be sure to mix an adequate amount of a wash before applying any of it to a sketch. Should the supply be exhausted before an area is completely covered, the wash already on the sketch will dry while a second batch is being mixed. Even if the two washes are mixed exactly alike, it is still most unlikely that the beginner can combine a wet and a dry wash without showing the junction between the two.

Study the penciled sketch for a moment and plan the order of its painting. It is known from the very nature of transparent water colors that a light wash can be overpainted with a more saturated or darker paint without difficulty and that a light wash can be made progressively darker by repeated applications of the same wash. It is also known that if any area is to appear white or near-white, this effect must be achieved by letting the white of the paper show. These facts help determine which parts of the sketch should be painted first, and which should be left to be painted last.

Normally the broader and lighter colored expanses of background are painted first. In a setting for the interior of a room, these expanses would be the wall areas, the ceiling, and possibly the floor. Start with the walls and paint each section or plane of the room separately. This permits time to guide and control a wash over a small area, without overpainting those spaces to be occupied by door, windows, or hanging pictures which will be another color. Move progressively around the set, painting the stage right wall first, then the back wall, and finally the stage left wall. As the washes are being applied, do not hesitate to turn the sketch from one side to the other or even upside down, if it is easier to control the flow of the washes or simply easier to paint with the sketch in that position.

The ceiling is usually painted next. It is not likely to present a problem since it is generally an unbroken expanse of a single hue. Although the constructed ceiling may actually be painted lighter than the walls of the set, the sketch of the ceiling should be painted about the same degree of brilliance as the walls since this gives the effect of the unlighted, shadowy, upper parts of a room.

When painting the floor area, be careful not to paint those spaces which are to be occupied by furniture. This is especially true if the upholstery of the furniture happens to be lighter than the color of the floor covering. Just how important the color of the stage floor will be to a design depends upon the sight lines from the auditorium to the stage. In a theatre where the orchestra level is low, very little of the stage floor will be seen. In such cases the color of the floor covering can be minimized by using a plain rug in a neutral color or perhaps by using nothing other than the dark brown canvas floor cloth. Should sight lines from the auditorium and balcony give the audience a good view of the floor, an excellent opportunity is provided to use a painted floor cloth. Floor cloths made of heavyweight muslin are not expensive and, because they can be repainted several times, their initial cost can be prorated over several productions.

Doors, windows, and special architectural features of the set are painted at the same time as the furniture. These features, especially the furniture and possibly some of its upholstery, are likely to be the darkest and most saturated colors used in the setting; consequently, they are the last items in the sketch to be painted.

Before painting give some thought to the source of light within the setting and to the highlights and shadows the light will create on the furniture. Even in a brightly lighted room the furniture casts shadows on the floor or possibly on a wall. The effort spent on painting in these shadows is well repaid by the added three-dimensional quality they give to the sketch.

Some designers like to include the figure of an actor or two within the sketch as a means of establishing the size and scale of the setting. This practice is acceptable for those who can draw the human figure in some recognizable form. However, it is not really necessary when the design includes standard-sized furniture or stairs, since these features do the same thing.

The final steps in completing the sketch are cleaning up the wide unpainted border, drawing in a narrow margin line around the tormentor plane, and printing underneath the picture the title of the play, the date and the name of the artist.

Sketches are sometimes given rough treatment by members of the production staff. Some of them seem unable to talk about a sketch without a pencil or pen in hand as they point out first one feature and then another of the setting. These enthusiasts leave a road map of scrawls and lines as a reminder of their comments. The sketch is also likely to encounter other hazards as work progresses. If it is taken to the shop to be used as a color guide for painting the setting, there is an excellent chance that paint will be smeared or spattered on it. It is a foregone conclusion that its border will be covered with dirty fingerprints. For these reasons, if there is any thought of saving the sketches after the production, they must be protected. Whether the sketch is done on water color paper and mounted behind a cardboard frame or finished on illustration board, it is wise to cover it with a transparent material such as cellophane or thin sheets of cellulose acetate. Wrap the covering over the face of the design and tape it in place on the back.

8

THE DESIGNER'S
PLANS

The colored sketch of a setting may be a thing of beauty and it may give a clear picture of the designer's intentions, but it does not give a technician the information he needs to build the set. A series of mechanical drawings, called the designer's plans, is filled with specific information which describes the set in great detail in terms of exact dimensions. These plans are prepared by the designer for the technician, and they consist of a ground plan, front elevations, detail drawings, full-scale drawings, and sight-line drawings.

The Ground Plan

The ground plan is the key drawing on which the remainder of the designer's plans are based. It is a scaled mechanical drawing showing the top view of a setting in position on stage. It clearly shows the form and size of the setting and its relation to the proscenium arch, curtain line, tormentors, off-stage space, and permanent stage equipment such as the bridge, cyclorama, and locking rail. The location and measurements are given for all architectural features of the setting such as doors, windows, fireplaces, columns, levels, niches, built-in bookcases, stairways, and landings—both on-stage and off. The position and measurements are shown for all backings, ground rows, cutouts, set pieces, wings, borders, and drops.

A majority of the work done in planning a production depends upon the information provided by the ground plan. During the rehearsal period the director consults it for information regarding the location of acting areas, entrances, and windows, or for furniture arrangements that might influence stage business. The lighting artist uses it as a basis for his light plot. It provides the property master with the measurements of available floor space and wall areas, which he needs for the selection of furniture of the proper size. The technical director consults it in planning the details of the method of shifting and to determine the amount of off-stage storage space required. The ground plan is used by the designer to establish satisfactory sight lines and to supplement the information contained in the elevations and detail drawings.

Before work can be started on the ground plan of the setting itself, it is necessary to have an accurate plan of the stage, and its equipment, on which the setting will be mounted (see Plate 32). A scale of $\frac{3}{8}''$ or $\frac{1}{2}'' = 1'\text{-}0''$ is usually satisfactory for this purpose. All structural features of the

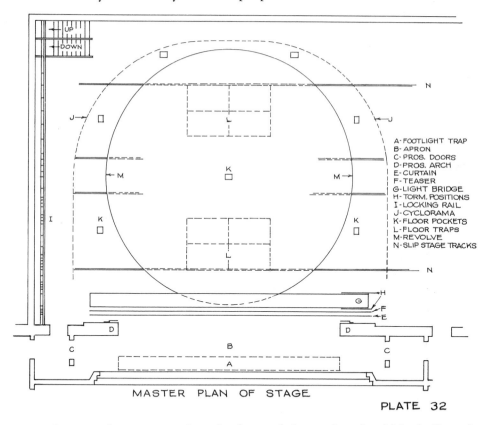

A- FOOTLIGHT TRAP
B- APRON
C- PROS. DOORS
D- PROS. ARCH
E- CURTAIN
F- TEASER
G- LIGHT BRIDGE
H- TORM. POSITIONS
I- LOCKING RAIL
J- CYCLORAMA
K- FLOOR POCKETS
L- FLOOR TRAPS
M- REVOLVE
N- SLIP STAGE TRACKS

MASTER PLAN OF STAGE

PLATE 32

stage that may in any way alter the form of the setting should be indicated. The stage plan will reveal the position of loading doors, dressing room doors, supporting columns, radiators, stairways, or any other features that must be kept clear of stored or stacked scenery. The apron, proscenium doors, proscenium arch, curtain line, and the normal position of the tormentors are always shown. The size and position of heavy equipment such as a light bridge, a slip stage (large wagons rolling on fixed tracks), a revolving stage, or elevators must appear on the plan. The exact location and size of stage traps and floor pockets and the position of the cyclorama must be indicated. The stage plan will also show the location of the locking rail and plot the position of all available battens. The more complete and accurate the drawing of the stage plan is, the more value it will have for the designer as he lays out the ground plan for a setting.

The time-consuming task of drawing a stage plan each time the ground plan of a setting must be drawn can be avoided by drafting a master plan of the stage on tracing paper and making a reserve stock of black and white prints. When the ground plan for a setting is started, a sheet of tracing paper is laid over a print of the stage plan, and any features of the stage that are pertinent to the problem can be traced with very little loss of time.

Prop your colored sketch where it can be seen easily, cover the stage plan with a sheet of tracing paper, and you are ready to lay out the ground plan of your setting. This first blocking-out is done freehand and all lines are drawn very lightly so that they may be erased easily. At this point considerable rearranging of the various features of the setting may be necessary until the plan faithfully presents the intention of the sketch. The first point to establish in this blocking-out process is the center line of the stage; locating this line simplifies the problem of balancing the setting with the proscenium opening. Next, establish the depth of the setting, the distance from the tormentor line to the back wall. The next step is to determine at what angle the side walls are to be placed in relation to the proscenium opening and to the back wall in order to provide the best possible sight lines. In poorly planned theatres it may be impossible to meet these sight-line demands without raking the walls to such a degree that the form of the setting seems distorted. Under such conditions it is advisable to ignore the extreme side seats. (Provision should be made to sell only those seats that provide a good view of the stage.)

After the depth of the set and the angle of the side walls is established, the placing of such features as doors, windows, stairs, fireplace can be settled. The size and spacing of these features should be exactly the same as depicted in the sketch, so that the same proportion and balance are carried over and incorporated into the ground plan. Poor placing of entrances and exits or even serious mistakes in the architectural plan of a setting—mistakes that were not detected in the perspective sketch—may come to light in drafting the ground plan. Such mistakes should be called to the attention of the director, and, if they are deemed to be important enough, the design should be changed to conform to the plan.

When the form of the setting has been blocked out to your satisfaction, all lines may be redrawn and made heavier. This redrawing is done with the aid of drafting instruments. All important over-all dimensions, the dimensions indicating the width and location of any structural features, and the dimensions necessary to show the angle formed by the setting or any of its parts should be shown on the plan. The reading of the ground plan can be made easier if you will remember to place the dimensions on the drawing in such a manner that they may be read from left to right or sideways from bottom to top. The dimensions should be complete enough to allow the stage manager or the technician to chalk out the position of the setting on the stage floor without having to apply a scale rule to the plan to find some missing dimension. Each unit of the setting, i.e., the side walls, back wall, backings, cutouts, and so forth, should be lettered or numbered for ready identification with the drawings of the same unit in the elevations and the detail drawings. When more than one copy of the plan is necessary, the drawing should be made on tracing paper and inked or very heavily penciled; any number of prints can be made from this original.

Some mention should be made as to why a *top* view of a stage setting is used in drawing the ground plan in preference to the horizontal sectional plan employed by architects in laying out the plan of a house. Since the walls of a setting literally have no thickness, except those special returns added around doors and windows, a top view is less apt to be misread or misunderstood than a sectional plan.

Front Elevations

It is necessary to supplement the information provided by the ground plan with another set of mechanical drawings, called the front elevations. They are a front view of the setting as it would appear if it were flattened out until it was in a single plane. The primary purpose of the elevations is to indicate all vertical measurements, which cannot be shown clearly on the ground plan. These would include such dimensions as the height of walls, doors, windows, and the location of the windows on the walls. The position, size, and arrangement of all built-in structural features such as cupboards, recessed areas, and bookcases is given on the elevations; and decorative features of the walls such as baseboards, chair rails, wainscoting, cornices, etc., also can be spotted accurately.

Of equal importance is the secondary purpose of the elevations. Here, for the first time, the designer has an opportunity to see his design after the sizes and shapes of its various parts have been determined. What appears on the elevations is a proportional reduction of what an audience will actually see. Matters of scale, proportion, and form on any and all parts of a setting can now be judged. If they are found lacking in any way or if they need readjustment to effect a better composition, the elevations are corrected to achieve the desired end. With each correction or adjustment made in the elevations, the ground plan must be altered to correspond to it. It cannot be stressed too frequently that the designer is actually molding and

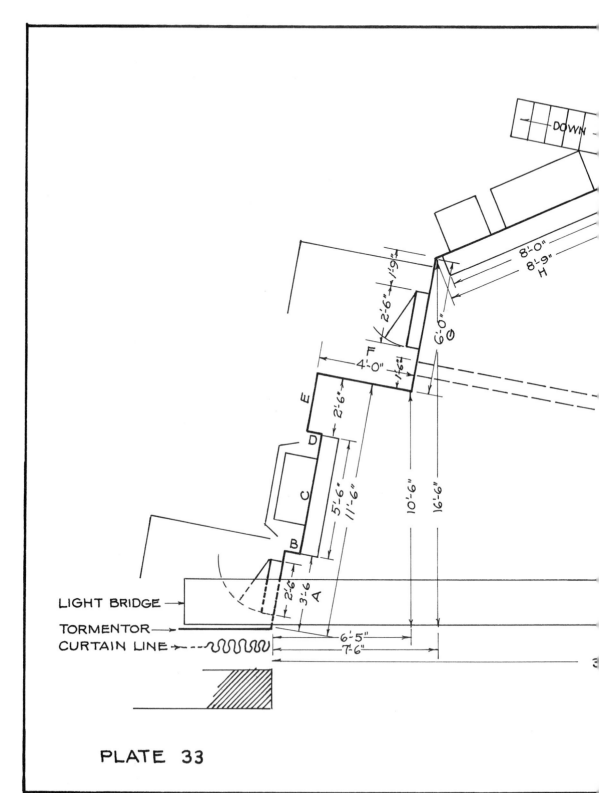

DOWN

8'-0"
8'-9"
H

2'-6"
1'-9"

F
4'-0"
1'-6"

6'-0"
G

E
2'-6"

D

C

5'-6"
11'-6"

10'-6"

16'-6"

B

A
2'-6"
3'-6

LIGHT BRIDGE →

TORMENTOR →

CURTAIN LINE →

6'-5"
7'-6"

PLATE 33

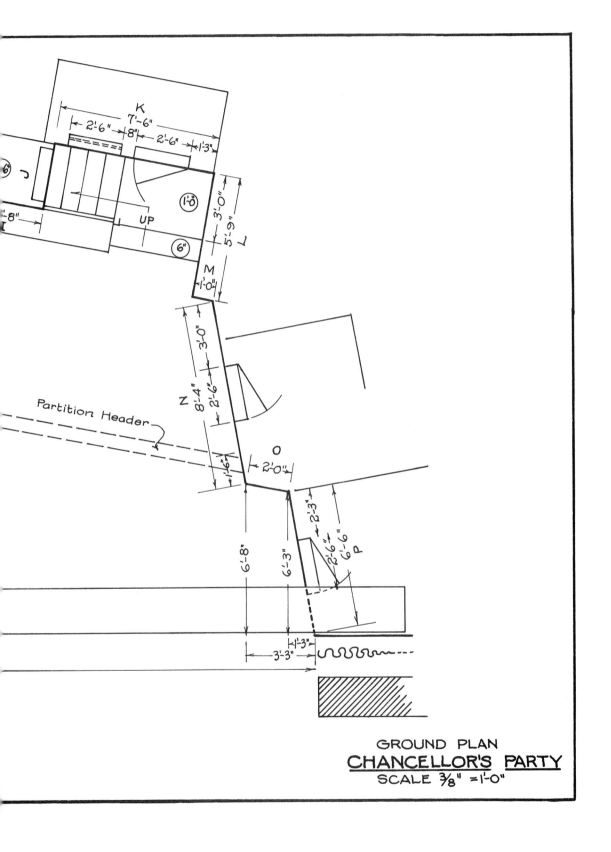

GROUND PLAN
CHANCELLOR'S PARTY
SCALE 3/8" = 1'-0"

forming his design at the very moment when he is working on the elevations. He is designing as much, or more, with his drafting as he was with
his thumbnail sketches and color renderings. This is perhaps the most critical
step in the realization of a design, for it is at this point that the dimensions
for all component parts of the setting are established.

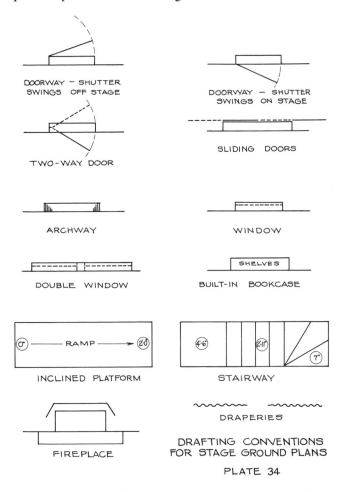

DOORWAY – SHUTTER
SWINGS OFF STAGE

DOORWAY – SHUTTER
SWINGS ON STAGE

TWO-WAY DOOR

SLIDING DOORS

ARCHWAY

WINDOW

DOUBLE WINDOW

BUILT-IN BOOKCASE

INCLINED PLATFORM

STAIRWAY

DRAPERIES

FIREPLACE

DRAFTING CONVENTIONS
FOR STAGE GROUND PLANS

PLATE 34

The elevations are usually made on the ½″ = 1′-0″ scale and may
require as many as two or three plates to show all parts of the setting
clearly. Lay out a clean sheet of paper on the drafting board and draw
in the heavy margin and title bracket. If care is used in determining the
spacing and arrangement of the drawing, the three walls of an ordinary interior setting can be drawn on a single plate of average size. Usually the
backings, cutouts, ground rows, drops, and similar elements in the setting
are prepared on separate plates. Determine the height of the flats that will
be used to represent the walls of the setting. Plan the spacing on the plate
so that it will be possible to place one section of wall directly above another,
with sufficient room left between the two to record the necessary dimen-

sions. Draw in four horizontal lines representing the distance between the tops and bottoms of the walls. Consult the ground plan, and, beginning with the units located at the tormentor on stage right, scale off their widths along one of the two upper horizontal lines already drawn. Erect a perpendicular line at each of the two terminal points thus connecting the upper two horizontal lines already drawn. The rectangle so formed will represent the face, or front view, of the stage right wall area. Draw within this area the structural features indicated in the corresponding wall of the ground plan. The junction between the side walls and the rear wall is usually shown as a single perpendicular line— as though a paper model of the setting had been flattened out. Where two planes of the wall join to form a corner or an angle, as would be the case with a fireplace jog, a single vertical line should be used. Where it is impossible to show the full dimensions of a section of wall without extending the drawing beyond the margin of the paper, an omission or break line is used. This drafting symbol indicates that the drawing does not scale the full distance designated by the accompanying dimension, that is, a section of the drawing has been omitted. Each unit of the setting must be lettered or numbered for ready identification with the same unit drawn on the ground plan.

Remember that the purpose of drawing the front elevations is simply to *describe* the appearance of the setting; they in no way attempt to tell a technician how to build it. For this reason no effort is made to indicate on the front elevations the width of the various flats that will be used to construct it. Planning the division of wall areas into flats is one of the duties of the technician. He would much prefer to make his own analysis of the problem and to execute his own set of working drawings from which the setting will be constructed. Any attempt to combine the front elevations and the working drawings into a single set of drawings lessens the clarity of both and greatly increases the chances of making mistakes.

Detail Drawings

Many features of a setting cannot be fully described by drawing them in top and front views alone. Three-dimensional objects normally require a third view to supplement the other two. Also the $\frac{1}{2}'' = 1'\text{-}0''$ scale used in drawing the front elevations reduces some of the smaller features of a setting to such a small size that it is difficult, if not impossible, to include all the dimensions and notes needed to describe them fully. This would certainly be the case with an elaborate fireplace or with a doorway transom made of intricate glass paning. Such objects are drawn to a larger scale than that used for either the ground plan or front elevations. These detail drawings may be drafted by using any one of the four methods of shape description described in Chapter 5—orthographic projection, isometric drawing, oblique drawing, or cabinet drawing.

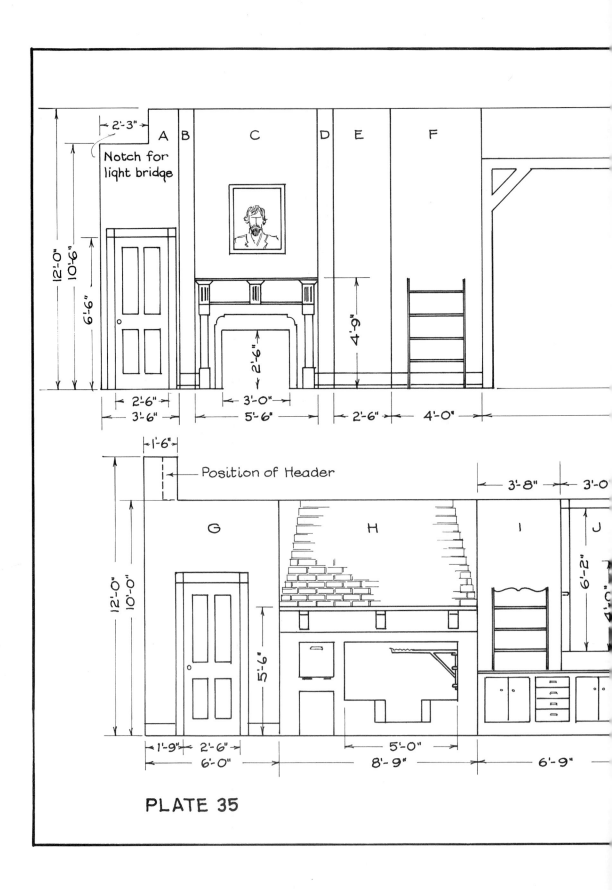

2'-3"

Notch for
light bridge

A B   C   D E   F

12'-0"
10'-6"
6'-6"

2'-6"
3'-6"

3'-0"
5'-6"

4'-9"

2'-6"
4'-0"

2'-6"

1'-6"

Position of Header

3'-8"   3'-0

G   H   I   J

12'-0"
10'-0"

5'-6"

6'-2"
4'-0"

1'-9" 2'-6"
6'-0"

5'-0"
8'-9"

6'-9"

PLATE 35

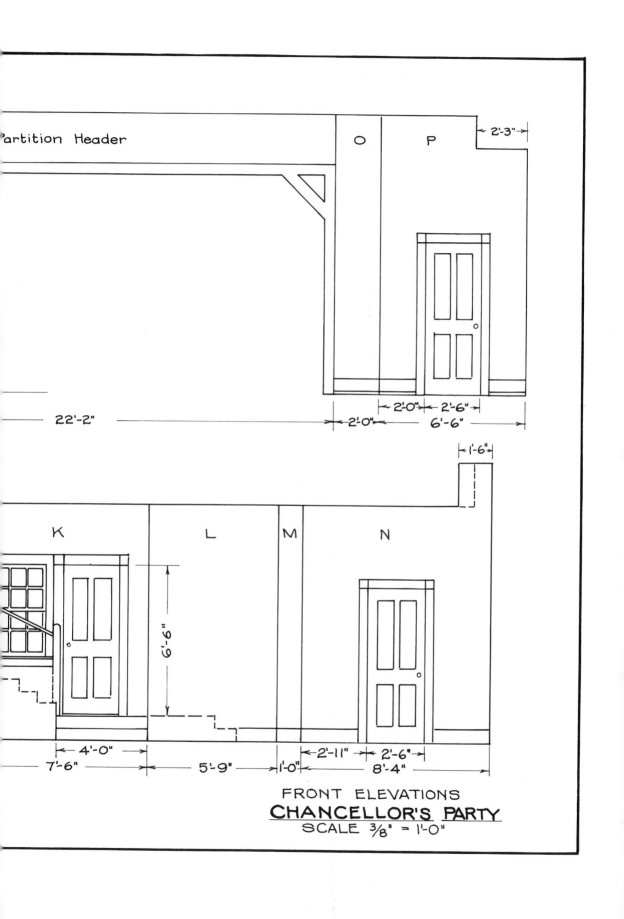

Partition Header

O   P   2'-3"

22'-2"   2'-0"   2'-0"   2'-6"
                      6'-6"

1'-6"

K   L   M   N

6'-6"

4'-0"   2'-11" 2'-6"
7'-6"   5'-9" 1'-0"   8'-4"

FRONT ELEVATIONS
CHANCELLOR'S PARTY
SCALE 3/8" = 1'-0"

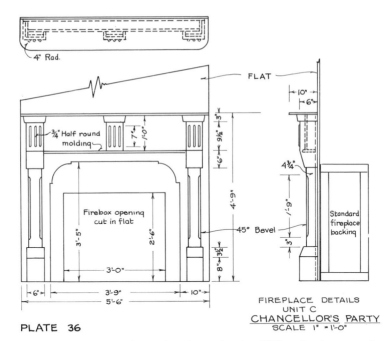

PLATE 36

FIREPLACE DETAILS
UNIT C
CHANCELLOR'S PARTY
SCALE 1" = 1'-0"

The question might logically be raised, "Why bother to draw it at all in the ground plan and elevation, if one must redraw it as a detail drawing? Isn't drawing it once enough?" It is not. The over-all size and shape of a feature such as a fireplace must be determined by seeing it in relation to its surrounding wall areas and to the other structural elements of the set. This can be done only by drawing it in front elevation. However, it must be redrawn to a larger scale and its third dimension must be shown to describe it fully.

Full-Scale Drawings

A few of the smallest features of a set are best drawn actual size. If the design is intricate or the object small, it is usually both easier and faster to draw to the full scale. This could well be the case with the pattern for a turned bannister or with the pattern for a wallpaper design. It is certainly easier to construct such an object from a life-size drawing than from one that has been proportionally reduced.

Sight-Line Drawings

There are few things so distracting to a member of an audience as having an important scene played on stage in a spot that is partially or completely out of his range of vision. Equally disturbing is the setting that is not properly masked, permitting the audience to catch glimpses of actors waiting for entrance cues or of lighting instruments and backstage paraphernalia.

Problems of this type can be anticipated and steps can be taken to correct them by checking the sight lines of a proposed setting at the time it is being planned.

Satisfactory sight lines can be determined by making two drawings of the auditorium with the set in position on stage—a horizontal sectional plan and a vertical sectional drawing. Because of the small scale required to show the depth of the house and the stage in combination, extreme accuracy will be necessary to assure satisfactory results. The horizontal plan depicts the exact position of a person seated in the extreme side seats of the first and last row of the auditorium. The vertical section shows the eye level position of a seated person (4′ above floor level) in the first and the last row of the orchestra; and if the theatre has one, from the first and the last row of the balcony. The third, or central position, represents the sight lines from the ideal seat in the house.

Fortunately most plays do not have the severe sight-line problems that were associated with an original play entitled *Mississippi* produced at the University of Iowa. The setting for this play (see Plate 37) represented a

MISSISSIPPI

PLATE 37

two-story river-bottom shack set on posts which elevated the first floor 2′-6″ above the stage floor. The second floor was 8′ above the first. According to the playwright, the flood victims, marooned in the house, were to be rescued from the second floor through a window located in the center of the back wall. Had this scheme been followed, a good third of the audience

would not have been able to see the action. In order to bring the rescue
scene into view both the design for the setting and the stage business
were changed from what was originally suggested by the playwright. A
sloping shed with a practical roof was added to the house on stage left.
A double window in the left wall of the upstairs bedroom made it easy
for the actors to clamber out onto the shed roof to await the arrival of the
rescue boat and to do so within full view of the audience. Both the vertical

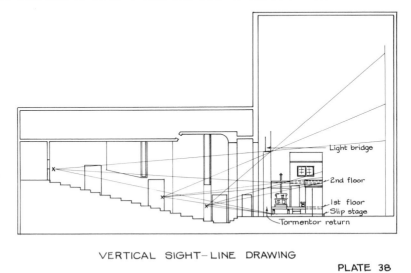

VERTICAL SIGHT-LINE DRAWING

PLATE 38

and horizontal sight-line drawings (see Plates 38 and 39) illustrate how
the setting was altered to meet the sight-line demands of the play.

The time expended on testing the sight lines of a set can be consider-

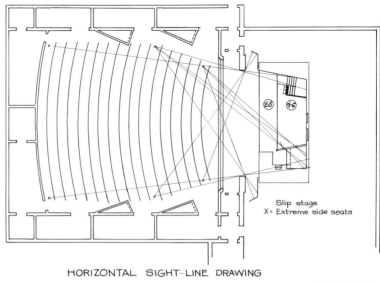

HORIZONTAL SIGHT-LINE DRAWING

PLATE 39

ably reduced if master plans of the horizontal and vertical sections are made into black and white prints similar to those made of the stage and its equipment. A drawing on tracing paper of the set in its proper position on stage can be placed on the master plan to check the sight lines quickly and easily.

The horizontal plan is used in establishing the angle of rake for the side walls of a setting and in determining the position and length of all masking backings. The vertical section is used in setting the height of the teaser and light bridge and in finding the required height of all masking units seen through openings within the setting proper. Whether an actor standing on a high platform upstage center can be seen by those in the last row of the balcony can be easily checked by use of this drawing. It is also used to find the height to which light battens must be raised in order to place the spotlights out of view of the audience, the necessary length of all snatch lines, and the height of high trim for all flown units of scenery.

The little time required to check the sight lines of a setting by the method just described is more than well spent. Too often the scenery is built, painted, and assembled on stage before the sight lines are properly checked. The sight lines may be perfectly satisfactory, but all too often it is discovered that some important entrance or acting area is lost to a good share of the audience, that the backings provided are too small, or that other masking units have been forgotten completely. The sight-line drawings will reveal shortcomings of this nature in ample time to modify them.

Models

Two types of models are in common use among theatre workers—the exhibition model and the working model. The exhibition model may be considered a particularly fine means of keeping a record of a production or it may be looked upon, as is so often the case abroad, as a decorative display piece for the foyer of the theatre. Such models are painstakingly constructed and are often masterly examples of the maker's cleverness and ingenuity. They are complete to the last detail of color and properties and may even be illuminated by colored light to approximate the hue and intensity of the actual lighting used during production.

The materials used in the construction of exhibition models are limited only by the maker's budget and his cleverness in adapting what is available. The nature of the design influences the type of material best suited to its construction. A few of the commonly used materials are wood, tin, plastic wood, balsa wood, clay, wire, cardboard, cellulose acetate, plaster of Paris, and a great variety of novelty fabrics.

The working model is in no sense a display piece; it is a rough, unfinished, three-dimensional mock-up of a setting as it appears in plan and elevation. It is made accurately to scale, but is usually left unfinished as far as properties and painting are concerned. This type of model becomes indispensable when the designs for a production involve complicated scene shifts. Technical problems involving limited storage space or stage equipment or the manner of assembling and shifting various units of scenery can be readily seen in the model, whereas they might easily be overlooked on paper plans. Problems in design that make use of forced or faked perspective are more satisfactorily solved by the use of a scaled model. This is essentially a trial-and-error method, but it permits the designer to see what visual effect his design will create before it is built and placed on stage.

PLATE 40   Scaled exhibition model of a Giuseppe Bibiena design, constructed by Sidney Spayde

The working model is a boon to the director, the designer, and the technician alike when they are confronted with a play demanding a setting that is highly irregular in form such as the mountain top for Maxwell Anderson's *High Tor*. Accurate plans of such a setting can show the general contour of the structure and give its height at various points, but such drawings are difficult to draft and to read. A much simpler and more satisfactory approach to the problem is found in a working model. Modeling clay is the best building material for this kind of model since it can be shaped into any desired form. Details of rock formations, the height of the various risers, and the angle of inclines can be established accurately. The director welcomes such a model, for in it he finds a much clearer picture of the acting areas and runways than can possibly be shown in a sketch or on the plans. The chances of his misunderstanding the designer's intention are reduced to a minimum.

When both director and designer have solved their problems with the aid of the model, it is turned over to the technician. Structures of this kind are usually made in sections to facilitate both building and handling of the scenery. The technician determines the proper division of the structure into sections, marks the sections on the model, and cuts them out with a sharp knife. The exposed face of each piece then serves as an accurate sectional view.

9

PAINT SHOP
EQUIPMENT

Organization of the Paint Crew

Organizing the paint crew is done in essentially the same manner for an educational theatre or a community theatre. Most often the designer, who is responsible for painting the scenery, must work with inexperienced helpers. No small part of his work is the effort and time spent in teaching fundamentals to his crew members. Usually this time is well spent since some of his helpers, who show a marked aptitude for the job, will progress to a point where they are capable of executing increasingly difficult assignments.

In educational and community theatre organizations the designer heads the crew. In this capacity he either mixes all scene paint himself or closely supervises this critical step. He determines the order of painting procedure and instructs his crew in the various techniques required in the application of paint. If the paint job is very complicated or if the painting technique necessary is especially exacting, the designer may have to do much of the painting himself. If the number of experienced painters at his disposal will permit it, the work of scene painting can be divided as follows:

1　Designer or paint boss. He is responsible for supervising all phases of painting.
2　Layout men. These men work closely with the designer; their principle duty is assembling and assigning to the crew those areas designated

by the designer to receive a given color or to be painted by a particular technique.

3 Fillers. The majority of the crew will serve as lay-in men whose duty is to do the priming, groundwork, and all large area covering.

4 Detail men. This is the most exacting work and it demands the most skill on the part of the painters.

5 Clean-up crew. Each member of the crew is responsible for cleaning his own brushes and paint containers. (The sooner this fact can be established, the happier all concerned will be!)

Color Elevations

If the designer is personally supervising the work of the paint crew there is little need for a paint guide other than that provided by the original water color sketch. Should the work of supervision and mixing of paint be turned over to a paint boss, it is advisable to supplement the information contained on the sketch with color elevations. These are large-scaled drawings, made on illustration board, which show the parts of a setting scheduled to receive a particular color applied in a particular manner. They are essentially nothing but samples of colors and painting techniques which have been made large enough for easy reading. Because of their similarity to scene paint, opaque water colors are frequently used in place of transparent pigments. Notes regarding the proportion of pigment used to obtain a particular hue should accompany these elevations.

Graphed Elevations

When the subject of a design is irregular in form such as a drop for a woodland scene or a whimsical stylized street scene, the design is difficult to transfer from a scaled drawing to full-scale scenery by means of dimensions alone. This transfer can be made accurately by employment of graphed elevations. Since elevations are already drawn to scale, probably $\frac{1}{2}''$ or $\frac{3}{4}'' = 1'\text{-}0''$, it is an easy matter to divide the elevation into $2'$ squares (see Plate 41). Draw in the horizontal and vertical lines with a colored pencil and number the spaces consecutively for ready identification. After the drop or cutout has been built, it is also marked off, by a chalk line, into $2'$ squares; these squares, of course, correspond to those on the elevation. The outline of the design can now be transferred by noting the points of contact between the contour lines of the design and the graph lines on the elevations, finding the corresponding points on the scenery, and drawing in free-hand the resulting enlargement of the design. It is gratifying and surprising to see how accurately and rapidly a design can be transferred by this method.

A slide and a projector can be used to transfer a design to scenery, but

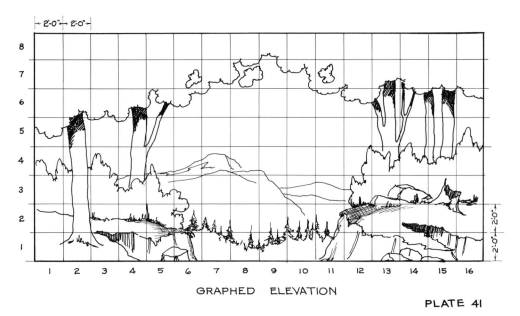

GRAPHED ELEVATION

PLATE 41

conditions must be almost perfect if the transfer is to be successful. The design must first be made into a slide which will produce a sharp, clear image. The lens of the projector must have the proper components to throw an image large enough to cover the desired area of scenery. Disadvantages of this technique are that no light other than that provided by the projector can be used without obliterating the image and that the designer must stand in his own shadow as he traces the outline of the design onto the scenery.

Paint Shop Layout

It is not necessary to have an elaborately laid out scene shop or to make a large investment in painting equipment in order to do a good job of scene painting. This statement has been amply proved by the work done in many colleges and community theatres where good shop facilities are lacking. Armed with nothing but a sound knowledge of scene painting, a few good brushes, some scene paint, and room enough to stand at least part of a set upright, these nonprofessional scene painters have turned out some remarkably well-executed settings. However, there is no denying that the same quality of work could have been done with greater speed and greater ease had the crew been working under better shop conditions.

The ideal paint shop for an educational or community theatre should be located at one end of the scene shop. Such an arrangement reduces the handling of scenery necessary to transport it from one shop to another. It also permits one person to supervise both painting and construction, a practice followed frequently in such theatres. The space allotted to painters within a scene shop should not be crowded or tucked back into a corner with a low ceiling. Ideally, there should be sufficient space along one wall of the shop to stand the walls of a full setting against it, placed end to end. There should be adequate floor space for all the three-dimensional free-standing units of a setting. There must be space reserved for mixing tables, sinks, paint bins, and paint containers. Adjacent to the painting area, there should be two small scene docks to be used for storing scenery that is waiting to be painted and that which is already finished.

Basic Equipment

COUNTERBALANCED PAINT FRAME

A device that completely eliminates any hazard caused by painting from ladders and one that is the greatest space saver in a paint shop is the counterbalanced paint frame (see Plate 42). It is a scaffolding made of $1\frac{1}{4}''$ × 6″ white pine, about 16′ to 18′ high, and, ideally, long enough to accommodate the side walls and back wall of a setting. The scenery rests upon a projecting ledge at the bottom of the frame and is nailed to the vertical frame. The frame and its load of scenery is lowered through an 18″ slot in the floor until the painters can reach the top of the flats while standing on the shop floor. The frame is supported by a series of $\frac{1}{4}''$ wire ropes that run through loft blocks to a head block and are tied off to a counterweight arbor. The weight of the frame is permanently counterbalanced by weights placed in the arbor. The frame, and the additional weight of the scenery attached to it, is raised or lowered by a $\frac{3}{8}''$ steel cable attached to the bottom of the arbor and running to the drum of a motor-driven winch that is anchored to the shop floor. Automatic stop switches halt the movement of the frame at predetermined heights. Casters mounted on iron brackets are fastened to the back of the frame and roll against the wall to prevent the frame from swinging when painters are at work. If there are any windows in the wall against which the frame is installed, they should be covered by removable plugs or shutters to keep light from shining into the faces of the working crew members.

STATIONARY WALL FRAME

For paint shops not equipped with a movable counterbalanced frame, a stationary frame will serve as a good substitute. A series of 2″ × 2″ horizontal wooden battens, placed 3′-6″ to 4′-0″ apart, are attached to an unobstructed wall area. The scenery is nailed to these battens in much the same manner as it is to the movable paint frame, but painting the upper parts of the set must be done from a boomerang or from ladders.

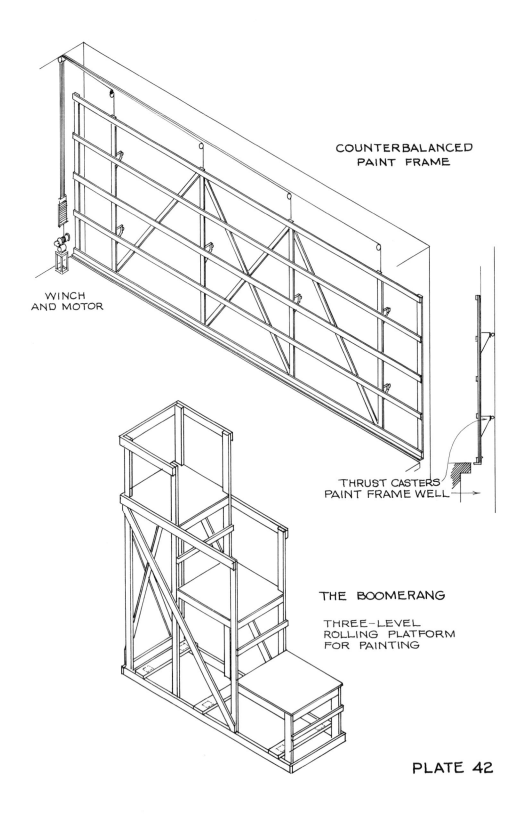

COUNTERBALANCED
PAINT FRAME

WINCH
AND MOTOR

THRUST CASTERS
PAINT FRAME WELL

THE BOOMERANG

THREE-LEVEL
ROLLING PLATFORM
FOR PAINTING

PLATE 42

BOOMERANG

The boomerang is a two- or three-level rolling platform from which two or more workmen can paint at one time (see Plate 42). The upper working level is high enough so that a painter can easily reach the top of standard-height stock scenery. The remaining levels are spaced so as to permit the painters to overlap their work and to provide each with enough floor space to store his painting equipment and still move about safely.

Although the boomerang is a large piece of equipment and takes up valuable shop space, it provides a much faster and safer method of painting than working from ladders. Furthermore, its usefulness is not limited to painting alone. There is one at the University of Iowa that has been used to good advantage as a portable rigging platform, a multilevel light tower, and an impromptu off-stage stairway.

LADDERS

No matter how well equipped the paint shop may be, some painting will have to be done from ladders. The author's experience has convinced him that the wide-based A-ladder is safest and most stable. Since both sides of this ladder are identical, two painters may use it at one time. Two A-ladders may be set at some distance apart and used with an extension plank for wide area painting. It is possible, though maybe not advisable, for a painter to lock one leg in back of the round rungs of an A-ladder in such a way as to free both his hands for painting. This cannot be done with the wide treads found on most step ladders. A gallon fruit or vegetable tin converted into a paint container can, by the addition of a hook made from heavy gauge wire, be attached to the rung of an A-ladder. The paint bucket rests solidly on one rung with the hook engaging the rung immediately above.

MIXING TABLES AND SINK

Indispensable parts of the paint shop's equipment are the mixing tables, hot and cold running water, and a sink. If possible, these should be located under a window to obtain the maximum amount of daylight for the critical job of mixing paint. The sink should be deep and large enough to permit a 3-gallon bucket to be placed beneath the faucet without tipping. Both hot and cold water should be vented through a pivoting mixing faucet. Since waste paint is disposed of by diluting it with hot water and allowing it to drain away, the sink trap should be large and accessible for cleaning. The mixing tables should be covered with copper or aluminum sheeting to protect their wooden tops. They should be placed on either side of the sink. Spilled paint and water will drain to the sink if the tops of the mixing tables slant toward it slightly. Beneath the table tops shelves should be built for the storage of buckets and cans used as paint containers.

PAINT BINS

The kind of paint bin used for the storage of dry pigments depends to some extent on the space available for the purpose. The bins should be large enough to hold 25 or 30 pounds of pigment, and each bin should have a fitted top to keep out shop dust. If wall space is available near the mixing table area, permanent tilt-top bins can be constructed. These bins do not have fitted tops, but they fit smoothly into a rack and are dust free when closed. Each bin is hinged at the bottom so that it can be opened by pulling the top outward; the rack has a simple lock that prevents the bin from tipping all the way out and closes it automatically after use. The angle of the bottom of an open bin makes it easy to scoop up the last vestiges of paint. An alternate type of paint storage container can be made at less cost by constructing a rack that will hold at an angle several 20-gallon garbage cans (17″ in diameter, 24″ high) with fitted tops.

When wall space is not available for a rack in a fixed position, the same rack can be built on a castered supporting frame and rolled out of the way when not in use (see Plate 43). Well-ventilated cupboards with doors that

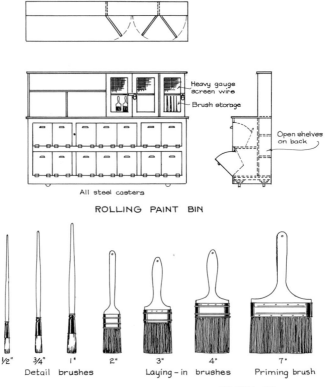

ROLLING PAINT BIN

½″   ¾″   1″   2″   3″   4″   7″
Detail brushes   Laying-in brushes   Priming brush

PLATE 43

can be locked should be constructed above the paint bins; paint brushes can be hung to dry in the cupboards. Open shelves on both sides of the cupboards can be used for storage of dyes, bronzing powders, spray paint, and other small supplies.

BRUSHES

The most important single piece of equipment in the paint shop is a good paint brush. It is true that almost any old brush can be used to smear paint, but it is also true that about the same effect can be obtained with a mop or with rags tied around the end of a stick. However, good scene painting demands good brushes. The best scenic paint brushes, designed especially for use with water-soluble paint, are 100 percent bristle. Bristles are long and have a marked degree of spine or springiness. Such brushes are not handled by most local paint stores but must be bought direct from scenic supply houses. These brushes are expensive, but if given the care they deserve, they will outlast cheaper brushes many times.

Three cardinal rules to follow in keeping a scenic paint brush in good working condition are: clean thoroughly in water after each use, store properly, and avoid the use of oil paint. Water-soluble paint dries rapidly. Therefore, a brush should be cleaned immediately after it has been used or some pigment will dry near the base of the ferrule, forcing the bristles to flare out at the tip of the brush. Rinse the brush and agitate the bristles under running water until no trace of color can be seen. Shake out excess water, and while the bristles are still damp, shape them until a flat chisel edge is reestablished. Remember that bristles will retain the shape in which they dry.

A small hole drilled in the tip of a brush handle will permit it to be stored by hanging it from a hook in a well-ventilated cupboard. In this position the bristles will dry rapidly and their shape will be undisturbed.

There is always some demand around a theatre for brushes that can be used in oil paint. No matter how carefully a water color brush is cleaned, it will never be the same after it has once been used in lacquer, shellac, enamel, or any other oil-based paint. Avoid the certainty of ruining a good water color brush by having on hand a few brushes that are especially marked and reserved for use in oil paint.

Three types of brushes are used in scenic work—the priming brush, the laying-in brush, and the lining or detail brush (see Plate 43). Priming brushes are 6″ to 8″ wide and are used for applying sizing and for all wide area coverage. Because of their size, paint can be applied very rapidly with them, but when they are charged with paint they are likely to be too heavy and unwieldy for anyone but an experienced painter to handle. Laying-in brushes range in width from 3″ to 5″, with the 4″ brush being the preference of most painters. By far the greatest amount of painting done in a scene shop is done with a brush of this type and size. A detail brush has a long handle and ranges in width from ¼″ to 3″. The best detail brushes have white bristles held in place by copper ferrules. They are used for painting architectural trim, all small detail work, and lettering. Great care must be exercised in cleaning and reshaping the bristles of these small brushes to prevent the bristles from gathering into clusters. Once this has occurred, there seems to be little that can be done to reclaim the brush for future use.

PAINT CONTAINERS

It will sometimes seem that the greatest boon possible to a designer or a paint boss is having on hand enough vessels in which he can mix paints so that he does not have to clean from a bucket a paint that he may need again.

There are a few simple requisites that such vessels must meet to be suitable for scenic work. Their bases should be wide enough so that the vessels will not tip over easily. The vessel should not have an overhanging inside rim, since the rim makes cleaning the vessel difficult. The mouth of the container should be wide enough to receive the largest of the laying-in brushes.

Large quantities of paint are best mixed in 2½- or 3-gallon buckets. One 3-gallon bucket, filled with paint, is usually enough to cover an average-sized interior with a single coat of paint. Large quantities of paint can be mixed in two or more buckets, but the paint must be thoroughly intermixed by pouring it from one bucket to another until the paint in all buckets is identical in hue. This process is called "boxing."

Most of the containers used for smaller quantities of paint can be obtained at little or no cost. Many restaurants receive their "fresh" fruits and vegetables in 1-gallon tin cans which make ideal paint containers. Providing each crew member with his own supply of paint in a gallon can will avoid the congestion, spilled paint, and delay that is likely to occur if all crew members are attempting to paint from a single large bucket. Fitted with a wire hook, the 1-gallon container is also just the right size to be used for ladder work. Wide-mouth coffee cans are useful for smaller measures of paint. Still smaller amounts of a variety of paints can be distributed in the different compartments of a muffin tin. Some scene painters fill the compartments of a muffin tin with different colored dry pigments and use it in much the same fashion as they would a box of dry pan colors—a brush is dipped in sizing water, touched to the dry pigment, and then mixed to painting consistency by working it on a palette made from a scrap of beaverboard. A can of clear water is also needed to wash the brush between charges of paint.

ROLLING PAINT PALETTE

A great improvement over the scrap of beaverboard and the muffin tin is the rolling paint palette (see Plate 44). It is used for the same purpose, but has the following advantages: it has a larger mixing surface, it carries a greater variety of colors, it is stable, it provides a worktable of convenient

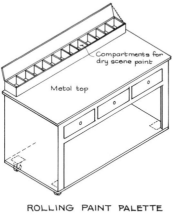

ROLLING PAINT PALETTE

PLATE 44

height, and it can be easily moved. It is a mixing table, mounted on swivel casters, that can be rolled to any position in the shop or on stage where detail or touch-up painting is to be done. The top, covered with copper or aluminum sheeting, is used as a mixing palette for small quantities of paint. At the back and along its length is a series of small covered compartments, each capable of holding about a quarter of a pound of dry scene paint. Beneath the top are two or three drawers for the temporary storage of brushes and other painting equipment. An open shelf beneath the drawers can carry large paint containers. The size of the table may vary, but one that stands 2'-6" from the floor, with a top measuring 4' x 2', will be adequate for most purposes and will not take up much floor space.

STRAIGHT EDGE

The straight edge is to the scene painter what a T square is to a draftsman. All straight line work used in painting architectural trim is done with the aid of a straight edge. It may be purchased from a theatrical supply house for about $3.00, or it can be made in the shop for a fraction of that amount. The straight edge should be 6' long, about 2½" wide, and from ½" to ⅝" thick. A block of wood or a screen-door handle attached to the center makes a straight edge much easier to control. The underside of its length should be beveled to stop paint from running beneath it and being smeared on the face of the scenery. Be sure to sand the beveled edge to remove any rough spots or splinters that might snag one of the bristles of a lining brush, thus causing a blot or a variation in the width of a line. When the 6′ straight edge is too long to be used, for example, when working in tight corners, shorter straight edges, 2′ or 3′ long can be used.

The secret of painting a perfectly straight line that does not vary in width is in holding the brush at a right angle to the canvas and in taking full advantage of the spine of the bristles by allowing only their tips to come in contact with the canvas as the brush is guided along the length of the straight edge.

CHALK LINE

Long, perfectly straight lines can be marked off rapidly by the use of a chalk line. The chalk line is a twisted cotton line about ⅛″ in diameter, charged with chalk, charcoal, or dry scene paint. The coloring agent is held in a small square of muslin and rubbed into the line. The line is placed against the scenery and stretched between two nails or pulled taut by two crew members. The center of the line is then pulled away from the scenery and allowed to snap back against it. This leaves a clear, sharp line imprint. Do not use the blue chalk normally used by carpenters for chalk lines, because it is difficult to paint over.

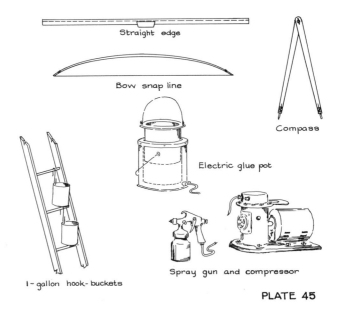

Straight edge

Bow snap line

Compass

Electric glue pot

Spray gun and compressor

1 - gallon hook - buckets

PLATE 45

A variation of the chalk line, the bow snap line, is handy for use on small units of scenery or in confined spaces. A line is stretched between the ends of a resilient piece of wood, between 5′ and 6′ in length, forcing the wood to bow slightly. The line is charged with dry scene paint, placed against the scenery, and snapped.

COMPASS

A wooden compass with arms at least 2′ in length is needed for drawing arcs and circles, for transferring measurements, and for division. The compass can be built from two 2′ lengths of 1″ x 2″ wood, tapered as indicated in Plate 44. The two arms are bolted at the top with a single ¼″ carriage bolt, washer, and wing nut. In the tip of the marking arm drill a hole just large enough to receive a piece of chalk or charcoal. Make a saw kerf through the end of the arm to bisect the hole and to extend the full depth of the hole. A rubberband wrapped several times around the tip will exert enough pressure to hold the chalk in place. The pivot arm can be fitted with a nail or with a pointed pencil eraser, attached in the same manner as the chalk.

Larger circles and arcs can be drawn with a piece of wood, ¾″ wide by ¼″ thick, used in much the same fashion as a bar compass. A nail is driven through the ¾″ face of the slat at the desired radial distance from the pivot point. The slat is then rotated to mark the desired arc. A length of chalk line is sometimes used for the same purpose, but the tendency of the line to stretch makes it less accurate than the impromptu bar compass.

CHARCOAL AND CHALK

Both charcoal and chalk are indispensable for blocking out designs, marking off areas to be painted, and indicating measurements. They are superior to other marking media because they can be readily seen when used on painted surfaces and can easily be brushed off or overpainted.

SPRAY GUNS

It is possible to get along in the paint shop without a spray gun and motor driven compressor but they should be placed high on any list of desirable shop equipment. A motor driven compressor supplies the constant air pressure needed to make a spray gun operate. Certain types of painting techniques can be done much better with a spray gun and in a fraction of the time required to do them by brush painting.

An electrically driven, constant-pressure spray gun, with an assortment of different nozzles to control the shape of the spray, soon pays for its initial cost by the saving in work hours. It should be stressed that even the highest priced spray gun on the market will not give satisfactory results unless it is properly cleaned after each use. The paint container must be removed, thoroughly cleaned, partly filled with hot water, and reattached to the gun; the hot water is then sprayed through the gun to clean the inside of the paint duct, needle valve, and nozzle. The gun is then dismantled, wiped dry, and all working parts are lightly oiled to prevent pitting and rusting.

Inexpensive, hand-pumped spray guns have only limited use. They are hard to keep in working order and it is very difficult to control the spray. Most of the work accomplished with them is, therefore, spotty.

ELECTRIC GLUE POT

Glue is prepared for mixing with scene paint by heating it in a double boiler. This may be done by placing glue and a little water in a bucket and inserting this into a second bucket partly filled with water which is then placed on a gas heater or an electric plate. Half of a brick placed between the bottoms of the two buckets will prevent their jamming together. The only difficulty with this method is the excellent chance that the water in the double boiler will boil away allowing the glue to burn. There aren't adequate words in the English language to describe how offensive the odor of burning glue can be. Speaking as an old and experienced glue-burner, the author highly recommends the use of an electric glue pot. It is impossible to burn glue in an electric glue pot. Both of its vessels are made of copper, the heating elements are thermostatically controlled, and the glue is dissolved by heated air rather than by boiling water.

SCENE PAINT

Scene paint is sold in two forms, dry and wet. The dry pigments are in powdered form and will keep indefinitely without deterioration provided they are kept absolutely dry. The dry pigments are also the less expensive of the two. Wet paint is prepared in the form of a paste or pulp and is sold in gallon cans. Once a can has been opened, the paint may dry out and harden to such a degree that it cannot be used. However, some of the more unusual colors and the more saturated hues can be had only in pulp colors.

These pigments must be obtained through regular scenic supply houses; they should not be confused with packaged dry water colors sold at local paint stores. The two were developed for entirely different purposes. Scene paint is available in a much greater range of color, the hues are more saturated, and they were developed for the scenic artist who must paint over a variety of surfaces and with highly developed techniques of application. Household paints were developed for application over plaster walls or wood, the colors are more subdued, and they are usually packaged in small quantities. They also are more expensive than scene paint.

There are a number of excellent reasons why water-soluble paint is preferred to oil-based paint for scenic purposes.

1 It is less expensive.
2 It is noninflammable.
3 It dries much faster.
4 It is easier to mix.
5 It is much lighter in weight.
6 It is more easily cleaned from brushes and clothes.
7 It does not have a glossy finish when dry.
8 It may be washed from scenery to permit repainting.

BASIC COLORS

NAME	TYPE	CHARACTERISTICS	APPROXIMATE PRICE PER POUND
Light chrome yellow	Dry	Hue approximating primary yellow	.45
Raw Italian sienna	Dry	Rich tan; used extensively mixed with other colors	.35
French orange mineral	Dry	Saturated orange; heavy pigment requiring regular stirring	.55
Turkey red lake	Dry	Hue approximating primary red; must be cut with alcohol before mixing with water	.90
Venetian red	Dry	Exceptionally useful brick red; mixes well with chrome green to produce a good gray	.45
Burnt sienna	Dry	Rich reddish brown	.25
Raw turkey umber	Dry	Earth-colored brown	.30
Burnt turkey umber	Dry	Rich, warm brown	.30
Italian blue	Dry	Very saturated light blue-green; must be cut with alcohol before mixing with water; excellent for sky effects	.90
Dark chrome green	Dry	Excellent dark green	.45
French ultramarine blue	Dry	Intense color approximating primary blue	.45
Cobalt blue	Dry	Extremely useful light blue	.70
Hercules black	Dry	Jet black with excellent covering qualities	.45
Danish whiting	Dry	White pigment; large quantities used in raising the brilliance of any hue	.10

The catalogue of the Gothic Color Company of New York City offers a choice of colors from forty-six different hues. This list includes both dry and wet colors. There is no need to keep in stock all, or even a majority, of the colors offered. A carefully selected list of basic colors will allow the scenic artist to meet the needs of all but the most elaborate paint jobs. Special colors should be ordered as needed. A basic list of preferred colors is given in the accompanying table.

The basic colors will, of course, be augmented by each designer's personal preference in colors and by the needs of a particular paint job. A selection of additional hues is also listed in table form.

ADDITIONAL HUES

NAME	TYPE	CHARACTERISTICS	APPROXIMATE PRICE PER POUND
Yellow			
Primrose yellow	Dry	Strong brilliant yellow	.70
Milori yellow light	Dry	Similar to primrose yellow, but slightly darker	.70
Milori yellow medium	Dry	Strong, saturated yellow	.70
Hoyt's yellow lake	Wet	Saturated yellow, slightly transparent	.85
Orange			
Milori yellow orange	Dry	Saturated yellow-orange	.70
Orange lake	Wet	Very rich, saturated orange	.85
Tan or Buff			
French yellow ochre	Dry	Similar to raw sienna but more yellow and lighter	.25
English Dutch pink	Dry	Rich, warm tan	.45
Green			
Hanover green	Dry	Very light yellow-green	.98
Emerald green	Dry	Saturated yellow-green with less yellow than Hanover green	.98
Chrome green light	Dry	Good, inexpensive yellow-green	.45
Medium chrome green	Dry	Very useful medium green	.45
Malachite green	Wet	Saturated, very dark blue-green	.85
Saphite green	Wet	Excellent foliage green	.85
Royal green lake	Wet	Very strong, dark blue-green	.98

ADDITIONAL   HUES *(Continued)*

NAME	TYPE	CHARACTERISTICS	APPROXIMATE PRICE PER POUND
Blues			
American ultramarine blue	Dry	Not as strong as French ultramarine blue; good primary blue	.50
Celestial blue	Dry	Good, inexpensive, very dark blue	.50
Prussian blue	Dry	Almost blue-black; very strong; must be cut with alcohol before mixing with water	.98
Purple			
Violet lake	Wet	Slightly bluish purple; very powerful	.98
Royal purple	Dry	Excellent purple with a slight red cast	1.50
Purple lake	Dry	Similar to violet lake but warmer in tone	.98
Red			
English vermilion	Dry	Very saturated red-orange	1.50
Bulletin red	Dry	Similar to English vermilion but not as saturated	.90
Solferino lake	Wet	Excellent magenta color, a hue difficult to mix	.98
Magenta lake	Wet	Similar to Solferino lake but with less blue	.98
Turkey lake	Wet	Rich, blood red	.90
Light maroon	Wet	Yellowish red of low brilliance	.98
Dark maroon	Wet	Very deep brick red	.98
White			
Permanent white	Dry	Pure white with better covering qualities than Danish whiting	.40
Black			
Ivory black	Dry	Slightly transparent but an intense black	.45
Black lake	Wet	Jet black with good covering qualities	.85

Mixing Scene Paint

Contrary to the belief of many students, mixing scene paint is not a mysterious rite nor a complex procedure if a few fundamental principles are understood and followed. Perhaps the most confusing feature is the fact that scene paint changes color and drops in brilliance when water is added to the dry pigment. This need not be disturbing when it is realized that the paint will resume its original tone after it has dried. (A few test samples will prove this statement.) For this reason all scene paint should be mixed and tested for accuracy of tone while the pigments are dry. It is advisable to mix all the hues to be used on a set at the same time. This provides an opportunity to compare the hues for harmony and degree of contrast and to check them against the colors indicated on the color guide or the sketch. In mixing pulp or wet colors there is no alternative to mixing the pigments wet and testing the dry samples for accuracy of tone. A small dab of scene paint can be placed on a scrap of muslin or beaverboard and placed in the sun or held over a radiator where it will dry in a few minutes.

A second important fact that must be kept in mind is the painting consistency of the pigment. If it is too thin, it will not cover; if it is too thick, it is wasteful, difficult to apply, and has a tendency to flake off. No set rule can be given to govern how much water should be added to the pigment; the amount will vary somewhat according to the technique by which it is to be applied. For most purposes, however, it will be satisfactory if it has the consistency of thin cream or is similar to the viscosity of 20 grade oil.

Practically all scene paints are strikingly intense in color and are therefore seldom used in their saturated form. Usually, they are mixed with other pigments to alter their hue, to neutralize them, or to raise or lower their brilliance. Tints, obtained by adding whiting to the desired hue, are used with great frequency. Since whiting forms the base for so many hues used in scene painting, more of it is used than all the other pigments combined. It is advisable to keep this in mind when ordering a season's supply of paint.

It cannot be said too often that one must mix a sufficient amount of paint to complete a given job. It is difficut enough for an experienced painter to match a short supply of paint, and it is most unlikely that any other person can do it successfully unless he has kept an accurate record of amounts and proportions originally used—a precautionary step that is seldom taken.

THE BINDER AND SIZING WATER

A binder must be added to all scene paints, dry or wet, to keep the paint from rubbing off. The binder is purchased as a dry glue in granulated, flake, or cake form, and must be heated with water in a double boiler to convert it into a hot, concentrated glue. Flake and cake glues should be soaked in water overnight before heating in a double boiler. Granulated glue can be covered with water and heated immediately, but stirring helps to speed up its conversion into a liquid state.

The hot glue is added directly to the mixture of pigment and water in the proportion of about ½ cup to 1 gallon of paint. Should there be any question about the strength of the glue, test dry a sample of paint; if the paint dusts off on a clean piece of muslin, add a little more glue. Too much glue added to the paint will force the paint to congeal in the bucket and to be glossy or brittle after it has been applied to the scenery.

Some scene painters prefer to work with a sizing water which is mixed in the proportion of 1 part hot glue to 16 parts water. The sizing water is then mixed with the dry pigments, no other water being added. One advantage of this method is that it is impossible to forget the addition of glue. It seems very easy to forget the concentrated hot glue when it is added separately. On the other hand, a prepared sizing water will deteriorate in time; and it always seems to be kept in the very buckets needed for mixing paint.

CASEIN PAINT

There has been a tendency in the past few years to substitute casein paint for the more conventional scene paints. The characteristics of casein paint make it admirably suited for scene painting. It has remarkable covering qualities; one coat of casein is sufficient to produce an even, monochromatic base over a group of previously painted flats that vary widely in color. Using dry pigments with whiting as a base, two or three coats would be required to achieve the same result. Since pure casein paint does not need the addition of a binder, mixing it is very simple; water is added to it and stirred until it reaches the proper painting consistency. It has a pleasant odor. It will keep indefinitely if it is covered by a film of water and kept in a tightly covered container. Since it is water repellent after it has dried, it is ideal for painting scenery for outdoor productions.

Casein paint is most readily obtainable in paste form and may be purchased in quarts or gallon cans. White casein is sometimes sold in 5-gallon containers, a convenient size when extensive painting is being done. Twenty colors, in addition to black and white, are available. If a tint is desired, white casein and the tinting color are mixed to painting consistency in separate containers, and the color is added slowly to the white until the desired tint is obtained. Full strength colors or combined colors are mixed in the same manner but without the addition of casein white.

There are two limitations to the use of casein paint: it is expensive and its Fresco colors are available in a somewhat limited color range. Both disadvantages can be overcome in part by using casein white as a base and mixing it with conventional dry or wet scene paint instead of casein colors. The mixing procedure remains the same—mix the two separately to painting consistency and add the colored pigment to the casein white until the proper color is reached. The adhesive quality of casein white is adequate to bind the regular scene paint unless the amount of paint far exceeds the amount of casein.

Dyes can be used to color white casein in much the same manner as conventional scene paint. Some hues, such as orchid, a tint of cerise, or chartreuse, are difficult to mix by using scene paint, but they are readily available in dye form. The dye is dissolved according to the instructions and added to the casein white.

One final precautionary note—when a 5-gallon drum of casein paint has been opened, cover the remaining paste with a film of water and tightly re-place the drum lid, or the paste will dry out. There is no reclaiming that portion of the paste that has hardened.

10

SCENE PAINTING

The designer uses scene paint in much the same way and for the same reasons that an actor uses make-up. Through make-up an actor can accentuate certain features or make them less noticeable; he can materially alter his appearance to conform to the characteristics of a certain age level; and, to a lesser degree, he can give some indication of the state of his character's mental and physical well-being. What he does with make-up is the final step in the development of his characterization.

The scene designer uses color in a somewhat broader, but just as meaningful, a fashion. Color and its method of application are two important agents used by him to establish the age, period, and, in so far as possible, the country in which the setting is supposedly laid. He uses color as an instrument in his effort to create a visual effect which parallels the mood of the play. He may use color to attract attention to some specific feature of the design, and it is often by means of color that he adds variety and interest to his design. Color is one of the dominant parts of a setting; what it says to the eyes of an audience will be perceived even before the playwright's words are heard and comprehended. How paint is applied is almost as meaningful as the hue selected. If this truth could be instilled in those who design for the theatre, there would be a noticeable reduction in the number of flat, uninteresting, and lifeless paint jobs.

All scene painting is dictated by two principal requirements. First, it is necessary to exaggerate the manner of paint application if one is to achieve an effect that can be appreciated from a distance. Second, the effect of colored light on colored pigment must be considered in order to avoid some totally unexpected results. It can be easily understood that a spectator seated in the first row of the auditorium is separated from the back wall of a setting by the combined widths of the orchestra pit, the forestage, and the depth of the playing space. Small detail, fine lines, delicate hues, and subtle contrasts are lost to most of an audience simply because they are too far away. To overcome this problem scenic designers have resorted to an exaggeration of line, form, and color in the treatment of detail and in the techniques they have developed for the application of paint. A close inspection of these techniques reveals that the majority of them are characterized by a boldness of effect, a coarseness of application, and a sharpness of contrast that differs widely from methods used in any other field of painting. The most widely used painting techniques will be discussed in detail later in the chapter.

The best advice possible on how to find out what will happen to paint when it is seen under colored light is to test it. The variables that affect the results are so numerous that no accurate chart to predict the results can be constructed. There are no standard names for pigments or lighting color media; several spotlights, each with a different color medium, may be focused on the scenery in any number of combinations; some color media may have faded; the number of spotlights used and the intensity of their illumination will influence the color of the painted scenery. Add to these the almost limitless gradations that are possible through the mixture of color pigments, and it becomes clear why testing is the safest way to predict the effect of colored light on colored paint. Testing is done by viewing samples of a proposed color scheme under colored lights that duplicate those to be used on the stage. At this stage, corrections can be made either in the paints or the color media with a minimum of time and effort.

A few generalizations may be of value to those who have had little experience in judging the effect of colored light on painted surfaces. Very marked changes in the appearance of paint usually occur when both the pigment and the color medium are used in saturated form. If, for example, blue moonlight strikes the side of a red barn, the barn appears to be purplish black in color. The more neutralized a paint becomes, i.e., the closer it advances toward gray, the more accurately it reflects the colored light thrown upon it. Tints and deep shades of any hue are less likely to be changed by colored lights than clear, saturated colors.

Preparing Scenery for Painting

In nonprofessional theatre organizations it is a common practice to reduce the expense and time of building by constructing new settings from scenery already on hand. The stock scenery is, of course, altered and reassembled, and the old pieces may be supplemented with one or two new flats or special units. This results in the use of a motley array of flats—some old, some new, some patched, and no two of the same color. It is difficult to paint such a collection of surfaces with any assurance that the finished job will not be disfigured by variations in surface textures or by underlying colors that bleed through. The precautionary steps listed below should be taken in order to overcome these difficulties and to facilitate an even application of paint over all the scenery.

1 Patch all holes in the canvas. Cover a piece of muslin about twice the size of the hole with canvas glue and place it over the hole on the back of the flat. Pull the edges of the tear together on the face of the flat and smooth them down.

2 Paint over water or oil stains with a thin solution of shellac and alcohol. Serious oil stains should be cut out and the hole patched.

3 Tighten all loose canvas by painting the back of the flat with hot glue and water sizing to which a little cheap pigment has been added. (The pigment makes it easier to see which areas have been painted.)

4 In altering a window or door flat into a plain flat, try to find canvas or muslin that matches the condition of the covering material already on the flat. Otherwise, the difference between the surface textures of new canvas and old painted canvas may be discernible even after several coats of paint.

5 Apply dutchmen (strips of muslin covering the junction between hinged flats) with a paste composed of three parts cold water paste to one part hot glue. This mixture will not stain through the dutchman to darken the finish the paint job. Select material for dutchmen to match the condition of the covering material used on adjacent flats.

6 Flats covered with new canvas or muslin should be given one or two coats of priming to reduce the difference in texture between the old and new flats.

SIZING

Sizing is a preparatory coat needed especially when flat frames are covered with new canvas or muslin. The application of sizing accomplishes two purposes. First, by shrinking, it tightens the new covering material on the frames of the flats; second, it lays the foundation for the coats of paint to follow. There are several ways in which sizing can be made. If all the flats are covered with new material, the sizing can consist of whiting, glue, hot water, and a little inexpensive pigment that makes the sizing easier to see during application. If the scenery is made from stock flats which vary in color, a little formaldehyde or alum (about ¾ cup to 3 gallons of paint) can be added to the sizing to prevent the undercoats from bleeding through. Dye painting, used to achieve translucent effects, must be done on unpainted covering material with a special sizing made of starch. Laundry starch is cooked, then added to regular sizing water in the proportion of 1 cup of starch to 3 gallons of sizing water.

PRIMING

Priming is a preparatory coat of paint, needed especially when repainting old scenery, to provide a uniform surface for the succeeding coats of paint. It is normally made with a base of whiting to which has been added a cheap pigment which approximates the hue desired in the finished color. Priming also provides a good opportunity to use up all the old paint left over from a previous job. Assuming that the old paints have not spoiled and are not too saturated in hue, they may be mixed together and added to a base of whiting. Add to the resulting mixture enough of its complementary color to neutralize the hue and to produce a gray or brownish paint. Both colors are easily overpainted. Because of the greater covering quality of casein paint, the priming coat can be omitted if the succeeding coats are mixed with casein paint as a base rather than with whiting.

Painting Techniques

The basic techniques used in scene painting are simple in themselves, but they are as variable as the skill and ingenuity of the painter can make them. Even among experienced painters there is a noticeable difference in the results each will achieve, even when all are supposedly painting with the same technique. Somehow each painter manages to leave his own individual stamp on whatever techniques he happens to be using. The basic techniques are frequently combined to obtain a particular effect, and many of them are subjected to experiments and modifications that can lead to special innovations. How successfully a painter accomplishes this depends on how thoroughly he has mastered a technique and on his willingness to try for something new that may lead to a better, more expressive way of painting.

BASE COAT

This coat of paint is the foundation. It establishes, as far as possible with a single application of paint, the hue and brilliance desired in the finished setting. This coat must be mixed and compared carefully with the color sketch or the color guide. Apply the paint carefully by working from the top of the scenery toward the bottom with brushes that are well charged with paint. Do not scrub or paint over the same area. This is particularly important when repainting old scenery; the underlying paint may become moist enough to work through and discolor the paint being applied. Paint with long, easy strokes and use the flat tip of the brush rather than its edge. Organize the work so as to avoid having to stop a day's work with an area of scenery only partly painted. Arrange to stop where a natural break of plane is reached, such as the junction of the side and back walls. This precaution will eliminate any slight difference of tonal effect caused by paints standing overnight and not being thoroughly stirred before reuse or by too obvious a junction between paint that has already dried and that which is applied afresh.

No matter how carefully the work is planned, there will, however, be occasions when it is necessary to stop painting an expanse of scenery before a natural break can be reached. Joining the dry and wet portions without too obvious a junction can be helped by "feathering out" an area before stopping. Rather than stopping with a sharp brush stroke, gradually work all pigment from the brush onto the unpainted canvas as the painted area is extended. To join a fresh area to one that is already dry, start on an adjacent unpainted area and repeat the above technique, working back to the dry area and allowing one feathered edge to overlap the other.

SHADED BASE COAT

Effects such as the faded walls of a Victorian living room that has mellowed with age or the dark and dingy walls of a basement apartment can be made more realistic by gradually blending or shading the wall areas from one hue to another or by shading through different degrees of brilliance of a single hue. The careful shading of wall areas from top to bottom, in the corners, and around fireplaces and architectural trim will also relieve the uninteresting effect produced by a flat, evenly applied base

PLATE 46   Shading

coat. Shading of this type is generally done with two, or possibly three, different degrees of brilliance of the same hue. The shading may be subtle or very distinct, depending on the degree of contrast between the paints being used. The secret of a smooth gradation is the speed with which the paint is applied; it must be graded on the scenery while the blending colors are still moist. Be sure to use a separate brush for each graduation color or the difference in brilliance will be lost by the paints being intermixed on the bristles of a single brush. Work a small area at a time and move progressively around those portions of the set to be shaded. It is much easier to shade or blend colors when one is working on new covering material, since it retains moisture longer than old, heavily painted scenery. Old coverings have a tendency to absorb fresh paint almost as rapidly as it can be applied.

SPATTERING

The appearance of uneven or poorly executed blending can be improved by spattering over it with the same paints used in blending. Interlace the spatters directly over the blended area by extending a dark spatter over a light painted area and carrying the light spatters over the dark. This should be done with a very fine spatter allowing it to fade off beyond the limits of the shaded area.

Spattering is one of the fastest methods of applying paint to scenery. It has, in addition to speed, a number of other advantages which make it one of the most valuable and versatile methods by which scenery can be painted. It is used extensively for shading parts of a setting by blending from one hue to another. It may be applied over any type of base coat without obliterating it. It is used to change the tonal effect of a paint job that may be off hue, too bright, or too dull. Wallpaper patterns or detail work which contrast too strongly with the base coat can be toned down by an application of spatter. Novelty scenery which is to change color under lights is usually painted by this method.

PLATE 47   Spattering

To apply spatter, dip the tip of the brush (about the last 1½″ of the bristles) into paint and drain off most of the pigment. Stand about 4′ from the scenery and strike the ferrule of the brush smartly against the heel of the left hand. This forces the bristles to snap forward throwing particles of paint toward the scenery. Constantly move the position of the hands and the body to assure an even distribution of paint. The size of the spatter particles depends upon the type of brush, the amount of paint carried by it, the distance of the painter from the scenery, and the force with which the brush is struck against the hand.

It is recommended that the inexperienced painter practice spattering on an old flat before attempting to work on a setting. In spite of the first few awkward attempts, spattering is not difficult to master if the suggestions above are followed. It will not be long before the painter discovers that he can lay an even spatter on a flat without getting most of the paint on himself.

MASK SPATTERING

Wide-striped wallpapers, festoons, large geometric figures, or wood paneling can be done by spattering over masks that are placed against the face of a piece of scenery. The masks can be made from lengths of stock lumber in varying widths, from pieces of rope temporarily tacked to the

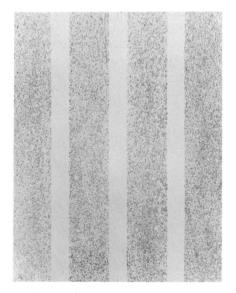

PLATE 48   Masked spattering

scenery in the proper position and shape, or from sections of building paper either pinned or taped to the canvas. Lines or forms produced in this fashion have the advantage of soft, indistinct edges that cannot be produced by a brush in contact with the painted surface.

SCRUMBLING

Scrumbling provides an area with a multihued base. It is a technique of painting similar to shading, but it differs from shading in that it produces an indistinct, all-over pattern rather than a progressive shading from one area to another. It may be used to good advantage as a base for certain types of wallpapers, for timbering, for several kinds of stone work such as marble or stucco, or simply to give an area a more interesting texture.

PLATE 49   Scrumbling

The variety possible with this technique depends upon the number of hues being used, the degree of contrast between them, and the manner in which they are blended on the surface of the scenery. The effectiveness of scrumbling depends upon blending the paints while they are still moist, and for this reason it is essential that scrumbling, like shading, be done as rapidly as possible. Permit each color to blend partly with the next, but make sure that some of each color remains identifiable as itself. Excessive blending can result in each hue's losing all of its identity, thereby producing a flat, monochromatic effect as though the colors have been intermixed in a bucket before being applied to the scenery. As a precaution against overblending be sure to use separate brushes for each scrumbling color.

Scrumbling can be done with various types of brush strokes—large or small circular strokes, straight or angular strokes, crosshatching, or irregular patterned strokes. A little experimenting with different kinds of brush strokes will yield a great variety of effects offered by this method of painting.

STIPPLING

Stippling is another method of applying particles of paint over a base coat, but the effect is heavier and coarser than that produced by spattering. It is accomplished by touching the paint-charged bristles of a large brush against the surface of the scenery. Old brushes are best for this purpose since their bristles have a tendency to form clusters; each cluster leaves its own imprint on the painted surface. Change the position of the brush before each contact with the scenery in order to avoid a repeat pattern. Sponges

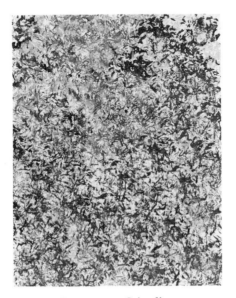

PLATE 50   Stippling

or coarse woven materials can be used in place of a brush if a lighter effect is desired. If natural sponges are used, it is advisable to split them open to provide a wide, flat surface for contact with the scenery. If excessive pressure is used to apply paint, the covering material will be stretched beyond the point where it can shrink back tightly on the flat frames. When stippling with a sponge be particularly careful that too much pressure doesn't cause a heavy deposit of paint along the edges of the stiles and toggle bars. This concentration of paint will reveal an unattractive skeletal outline of the flat. An annoying repeat pattern can develop from the imprint of a sponge as easily as if from a brush. To avoid this, rotate the sponge slightly after each contact with the scenery and overlap one impression with another.

DRY BRUSHING

Dry brushing is a very useful method for shading, for producing striations needed in simulating the grain of wood or timbering, or for overpainting blended base coats. To apply paint by the dry brush technique, partially charge the brush with paint and then remove most of it by wiping the brush against the sides of the bucket until the bristles cling together in small clusters. Draw just the tips of the bristles lightly over the scenery. A wide variety

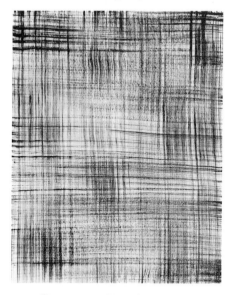

PLATE 51   Dry brushing

of effects is possible with this method of painting. For wood graining, it is recommended that some study be given to the patterns that are typical of the grains of different types of wood. These distinctive patterns can then be drawn in with the brush used in the manner described.

ROLLING

Rolling is similar in effect to spattering and stippling, but it produces a much smoother distribution of paint. Rolling is used to simulate rough textured finishes such as stucco, adobe, or plaster, and it also can be used to good advantage in giving texture to a simple base coat.

Fray the edges of a piece of burlap, about 20″ square, by snapping it briskly in the air until it has a fringe at least 1½″ or 2″ long. Fold the material into a triangle and double over the two corners so that all the fringed edges are on the same side of the burlap. Roll the burlap toward the point of the triangle, keeping the fringe on the outside of the roll. Dip the roll in paint and wring it out until it no longer drips. Apply the roll to the face of the scenery with just enough pressure to leave an imprint of the fringe and to make sure the roll doesn't slip. Change the direction of the roll with each contact to prevent the development of a noticeable pattern. An even distribution of paint can be obtained by using the same directional pattern as that used in crosshatching. Use a separate roll for each color applied.

PLATE 52   Rolling

CROSSHATCHING

Crosshatching is a method of painting accurately described by its name—brush strokes overlap each other at approximately 45° angles. Any irregu-

PLATE 53   Crosshatching

larities of the subsurface or of individual brush strokes are less noticeable when paint is applied in this manner.

PUDDLING

A rich textural effect can be obtained by a method of blending two or more colors called puddling. Lay the scenery flat on the floor and, holding two well-charged brushes of paint about waist high, shake the paint from them

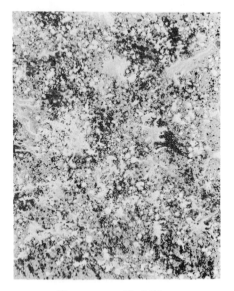

PLATE 54　Puddling

onto the scenery. Two or more colors may be blended in this manner but its success depends upon the nearly simultaneous application of all paints. This permits the paints to overlap, blend, and intermix while they are still in liquid form.

STENCILING

The application of well-planned wallpaper to a setting will probably give it more character and atmosphere than any other single painting technique. Actual wallpaper patterns are usually too small and too intricate for stage purposes. Therefore, a desirable pattern is usually reworked to enlarge and simplify it. This can best be done on a scaled elevation of some part of the setting which is to receive the pattern. Be sure to use a large scale for this work, at least a 1″ or 1½″ = 1′-0″ scale. This large scale permits the designer to work out the details of the pattern, its exact dimensions, the number of repeats required, and the pattern relationship. With these factors known, the full-scale stencil can be cut.

Commercial stencil paper comes in sheets approximately 20″ × 24″, which is large enough for most designs. Stencil paper is a stiff but lightweight cardboard, impregnated with linseed oil to make it almost impervious to water. A substitute for stencil paper can be made from Bristol board which has been given several coats of shellac or lacquer after the stencil has been cut. When treating Bristol board in this manner, be sure to apply the shellac to both sides of the cardboard and especially to the exposed edges around the stencil cuts; if the cardboard is not completely covered, the water paints will soften it and the stencil will fall apart. Reinforce the stencil by tacking it to a wooden frame made of 1″ × 2″ stock that has been butt joined on edge.

PLATE 55   Stenciling   PLATE 56   Stencil on frame

Most wallpaper patterns are laid out on vertical, horizontal, or diagonal lines. If these basic lines are laid off on the scenery to serve as guide lines, the time required for spacing, locating, and aligning the stencil positions can be greatly reduced. A chalk line charged with dry scene paint the same hue as the base coat, but a little lighter or darker as an aid to visibility, is used to snap off the guide lines. The stencils are laid over the intersections of the guide lines. What remains of the guide lines can be removed from the scenery by brushing with a soft cloth or a dry paint brush.

The fastest method to apply a stencil is by using a power driven spray gun, but it can be done by using a brush or by very careful spattering. In all cases, to prevent the possibility of smearing and dripping, the scene paint is mixed to a consistency heavier than for most other purposes.

Wallpaper patterns calling for more than a single hue can be applied in one of two ways when a spray gun is used. A stencil can be masked for each color, that is, all areas to be one color are sprayed at the same time and then the stencil is remasked for each of the other colors. Or, the complete stencil can be sprayed with the dominant hue of the design, and the accent colors painted by hand over the sprayed design. The advantage of the second technique is that the resulting design has enough variation in its repeat patterns so that it does not appear too mechanical.

Excessive contrast between stenciled patterns and the base coat should be avoided. Should this contrast appear too great, the patterns and the base can be toned together by spattering, rolling, or spraying over the designs with some of the base coat color. This breaks up the sharp lines of the stencil and reduces the contrast between it and the background.

APPLIQUÉS

Rough stonework, irregular plaster, adobe, and novelty effects can be done with appliqués. The scene paint is mixed with double-strength glue; to this mixture is added shredded asbestos, ground cork, coarse sawdust, chopped excelsior, or other similar material light enough to be held to the canvas by the binder in the paint. Since the consistency of this paint is much heavier than others, it may be necessary to apply it with a stiff, short-bristled brush or even with a wide-bladed putty knife.

Spackle, or spackling plaster, is sometimes used for rough textured surfaces, but it has the great disadvantage of adding a noticeable amount of weight to the scenery. It also has a tendency to chip off during a scene shift unless it has been applied over a solid surface such as plywood. Spackle can be purchased in any local paint store in a dry or a paste form. The dry powder is mixed with water and applied with a putty knife. It is pure white in color, dries very rapidly, and receives scene paint well.

BACKPAINTING

If new scenery, with only one or two coats of paint on it, is placed on stage so as to receive strong back lighting, it becomes almost translucent so that the audience can see the silhouette of the flat frames. This fault can be corrected by backpainting. Do not use left-over paints that are saturated enough to stain through the canvas and discolor a finished paint job. It is best to mix a medium to dark gray paint by using whiting and black. Paint lightly and rapidly over the back of the flats, being certain to work the paint close to the edges of the frames. The moisture in the paint may darken the paint on the face of the scenery temporarily, but there will be no perceptible change of brilliance or discoloration after the backpainting has dried.

DIPPING

The rough texture typical of some types of stone, tree bark, or sun-baked earth can be approximated by a method called dipping. The best covering material for this purpose is heavy muslin. The muslin is cut into small sections, 18″ × 24″ or 30″ dipped into paint, and applied to the flat one at a time. While the paint is still wet, the muslin is pinched, twisted, and folded into the desired shape and allowed to dry.

A variation of the dipping technique can sometimes be used to apply a dutchman that may have been overlooked by the building crew. Dip into scene paint strips of muslin, no wider than the combined widths of the two stiles over which they will be placed. While they are soaking, paint the area of the two flats where the dutchman is to be applied. Before this paint is dry, squeeze out any excess paint from the dutchman, and then apply it to the flats and smooth it down. There is sufficient glue in the paint to hold the dutchman to the flat after it has dried. Dutchmen properly applied by this method need not be tacked except at the top and bottom of the flat and around each hinge.

STRAIGHT EDGING

Painted architectural trim such as cornices, molding, and panels can be made convincing only by the use of a straight edge and a lining brush. A perfectly straight line is practically impossible to paint freehand, even for a professional scene painter. Hence mastering the use of the lining brush and the straight edge is a basic requirement for the craftsman who paints scenery. The straight edge is held, firmly enough to prevent its slipping, against the face of the scenery and with its beveled edge tipped slightly away

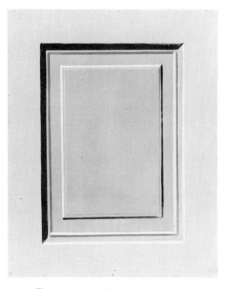

PLATE 57   Straight edging

from the canvas. This will help keep the scene paint from seeping under the blade and smearing. To ensure a long unbroken line that does not vary in width, the lining brush must be well charged with paint and the tip of the bristles must be worked into a flat chisel edge. As stated before, the secret of painting a straight line that does not vary in width is holding the brush at a right angle to the canvas and taking full advantage of the spine of the bristles by allowing only their tips to come in contact with the canvas. In short, paint with the tip of the brush, not its side.

STAINED-GLASS WINDOWS

Windows with simulated stained glass can be made in a number of different ways, but one of the easiest and quickest methods uses both opaque scene paint and transparent dyes painted directly on tightly stretched lightweight muslin. Windows done by this method are rugged enough so that they are not likely to be damaged in a scene shift. Such damage is almost invariably inflicted when color media are taped to a plywood cutout of the leading. Stretch the muslin tightly over the back of the window thickness. Outline the design in charcoal. Use a small detail brush and a dark gray opaque scene paint mixed with double-strength glue to paint in the leading; this must be a continuous line at least ½″ wide to prevent the dye from spreading from one area to another. As soon as the scene paint has dried, the areas so enclosed can be filled in with the proper dye solution.

GLAZING

Highly reflective painted surfaces are not usually found on painted scenery. The light they reflect is likely to prove distracting. There are occasions, however, when a slight gloss is desirable. An example might be the woodwork trim around doors, windows, and stairway of a supposedly smart interior. Such a gloss can be obtained by glazing, a process of covering a color with a thin, transparent wash which, when dry, will reflect more light than the uncovered color. Glazes can be made from clear shellac thinned with alcohol, from clear lacquer and lacquer thinner, from clear liquid wax, or from a solution of glue and water. As a precaution against getting too high a gloss, it is preferable to start with a weak solution and gradually to increase the gloss by waxing and polishing after the solution has dried. It is also advisable to test the solution on a sample of the color it is to cover, because a glaze may cause an objectionable change in hue or brilliance.

11

TOWARD AN UNDERSTANDING OF STYLE IN DESIGN

A Period of the Functional Theatre

Each of the great periods in the history of drama made use of visual backgrounds according to the needs of the plays, and around these developed staging conventions that were acceptable to the society that brought them into being. At first, as with the Greeks, very little in the way of scenery, as we think of it today, was either needed or used. The architecturally pleasing scene building stood before the open-air auditorium and provided the actors with their necessary entrances and exits and concealed them from the audiences for changes of costumes and masks. The theatres of this early period were not without their technical effects however. Pollux mentions some nineteen different devices by which the mechanical needs of each play could be met.[1] In two of these machines, the *exostra* and *ekkuklema*, are imbedded the principle of the present-day wagon and revolving stages; the *mechane* can be looked upon as the forerunner of our present-day flying systems. What little supplementary scenery was used in conjunction with their plays could be found in two other devices also mentioned by Pollux, the *pinakes* and the *periaktoi*. The *pinakes* were cloth-covered

---

[1] Allardyce Nicoll, *The Development of the Theatre*, New York, Harcourt, Brace & World, 3rd ed., 1937, p. 33.

wooden frames that could be painted and placed between the columns of the scene building to change the appearance of the colonnade into that of a solid wall. By leaving an open space between two of the columns additional but temporary entrances could be created. The *periaktoi* was a vertical, three-sided revolving unit placed at the extremities of the *logium*. The three faces could each be painted differently and turned to present a different "scene" to the audience. Actually, little else was needed in the way of visual backgrounds as the playwright placed in the mouths of his actors descriptive lines to draw verbal pictures of the play's environment. The point that should be kept in mind is that these mechanical devices, like the stages upon which they were used, were practical in nature, not representational.

The Romans, who borrowed so freely from Grecian art and culture, made few changes except to make the theatre building more elaborate. They made the stage deeper and wider. They reduced the size of the Greek circular orchestra to a semicircle and joined the scene building to the auditorium, thus making the actor-audience relationship somewhat more intimate. But as far as the use of scenery was concerned there was no noteworthy development.

From the time Aristophanes' first play was produced in 427 B.C. to the fall of the Roman Empire in A.D. 476 is a span of 903 years, but during these centuries the use of scenery, as we think of it today, remained a negligible factor in the production of plays. This is a period of a truly functional theatre. The architectural background provided by the *logium*, the *proskenion* with its graceful portals, and the projecting *paraskenion* walls was both stage and setting. Tragedies, comedies, and satirical plays alike were presented against this structure without benefit of any major alteration in its basic form.

A Period of Suggestive Backgrounds

The church stumbled upon a simple and effective device. It found that biblical stories and the lives of the saints could be made more meaningful to uneducated congregations if the stories were acted out. They further discovered that if the acting took place before a background that was suggestive of the story's action, it was even more easily understood. As simple as these ideas appear to us today, we must remember that they did not spring into full flower at a moment's notice. Their development was slow and gradual. It probably began within the cathedrals when the clergy first placed before the people a symbol of the sepulcher used in their presentation of the Easter plays. The story of Christ's death and resurrection was retold each year and with the retelling there came a gradual expansion of both the story and the manner in which the backgrounds were depicted. The symbolic nature of the sepulcher, the prison, a hell, and the other stations needed for these early mystery and miracle plays soon gave way to a more realistic treatment of them, and for the first time we find plays presented before settings that were indicative of the play's locale. Once the idea of a suggestive background had been introduced, it was only natural that further exploration of its use would follow.

The teaching of the scripture and the lessons to be learned from the lives of the saints had been difficult to impart when the only medium was the spoken word—preached in Latin. The church, in choosing to act out these incidents in the vernacular, had found a tremendous teaching aid. The interest it aroused in their congregations was reflected in the increased detailing of the story and the more elaborate manner of producing it. From this unpretentious beginning of the first liturgical play with its modest demand for just a few symbolic stations, these dramas developed to the point where some twenty-two stations were needed to stage the Donaueschingen Passion Play.[2]

For a number of reasons the clergy became skeptical of the good accomplished by the use of drama within the churches. The plays had grown too complex to be handled easily within the cathedrals; subject matter not entirely religious had crept into the scripts; and perhaps, too, the interest it aroused within the minds of the congregations was not completely devotional in nature. It was not surprising then that the church fathers, with increasing frequency and vehemence, issued indictments, restrictions, and prohibitions that kept the priests and lesser members of the clergy from participating in the dramas. However, the love of the festivals and of the drama had already been instilled within the people, and they had no intention of allowing these performances to cease. The town guilds took over the supervision of the plays, making them into semicivic affairs, with the acting being done by their own members. They appointed committees to look after writing the script, casting the play, and planning and constructing scenery. The scripts retained their religious theme, but also reflected a new rebellious attitude toward church domination. The whole tenor of the productions changed; the devil became a comic character, and the symbols employed by the church to establish the play's background gave way to more realistic suggestions of environment. The stations grew in detail and complexity. A triumph of the technician's skill was a station called hell-mouth, with ponderous jaws that were large enough to engulf a poor sinner and that opened and closed amid clouds of pine smoke and flame.

The drama had been in and out of the church. It was not as brief a journey as one might suppose from this survey, but a period of development measured in terms of centuries. It was in approximately A.D. 900 that the church first tried dramatic elements as a part of its regular church service, and it was in 1445 that the church ceased to sponsor the mystery and miracle plays.

---

[2] Nicoll, *op. cit.*, p. 67.

A Period of Two-Dimensional Reality

With the Renaissance came the third great period in the development of scenic design. Perspective and the proscenium arch provided designers with two devices that gave them almost unlimited possibilities with two-dimensional painted scenes. Behind the picture frame provided by a proscenium arch, the artist found that anything he could paint on a small canvas could be transferred to a larger canvas or drop, and thus placed on stage. The stage technicians kept pace with the designers and devised methods of hanging and changing these large paintings with ease and speed.

This period, like the functional and suggestive periods that preceded it, extended over several centuries. Roughly it spanned the period from about 1550, when Sebastiano Serlio introduced perspective to the stage in Italy, to the latter part of the nineteenth century. Actually no terminal date should be given for this period. The principle of the drop and wing setting is still being used in modified form, and it has its rightful place in the theatre of today for certain types of productions. It can be seen in the revival of period plays, where its use is almost mandatory; it has been adapted with great success for the fast changes required by musical reviews; and painted translucent gauzes, used for example in *Death of a Salesman* and *A Streetcar Named Desire*, are but drops in a modified form.

The introduction of painted backdrops cleared the way for an advance toward greater reality in backgrounds than had been possible in the theatre before. The changes that occurred in the painted perspective settings were of a mechanical nature, all aimed at advancing the knowledge of perspective, thus making possible more elaborate realistic vistas. A review of the designs of the Bibiena family will illustrate how completely the subject was mastered and how unbelievably complex the designs became. After the mastery of perspective, there came a period of conventionalism. Standardized settings such as "A Room in the Palace," "A Grove," "A Garden," or "A Prison" appeared with persistent regularity. These became stock settings and were used repeatedly and without alteration for plays of all types.

Toward the latter part of the eighteenth century an English designer by the name of William Capon came forth with the then novel idea that a stage setting should be directly related to the particular play for which it was designed. His "Ancient Palace of Westminster" and the "Tower of Londone" were based upon authentic source material, while his street scenes were flanked by houses adapted from picturesque Elizabethan dwellings. Philip Loutherbourg, another English designer, not only carried forward Capon's idea of a localized background as opposed to the old standardized designs, but brought to the stage an innovation in the treatment of perspective. He found that by abandoning the conventional two-dimensional drop and translating the design into terms of many set pieces that diminished in scale according to the laws of perspective he could create an illusion of greater depth than was possible with paint alone.[3]

A Period of Complete Reality

It was about the middle of the nineteenth century that the box setting appeared as an inevitable outcome of the steady advance toward realism. Many factors were influential in introducing this type of setting to the theatre. Not only were such men as J. R. Planché and the Duke of Saxe-Meiningen beginning to think constructively about the contribution a setting made to a production, but physical changes in the planning of theatres and advancements in the control and use of stage lighting helped establish the three-dimensional setting as a logical next step. Experimentation in theatre architecture had kept pace with that in scenic design and many were the plans and arrangements used for improving sight lines from auditorium to stage and for increasing the capacity of the house. The deep apron and proscenium doors that had characterized so many of the earlier theatres were now altered. The depth of the apron was noticeably reduced and proscenium doors were eliminated. The sloping stage floor, so essential for the drop and wing perspective settings, was leveled off, permitting scenery to be placed on it in any position. These changes had a pronounced effect on the actor-audience relationship. Previously, with the deep apron and adjoining doors, the actors had confined most of their acting and stage business to this area; the painted scenery served only as a background. Now, deprived of the apron, the actors were forced back into the setting; they no longer acted before it, but within it.

With the actors performing inside the setting and with brighter stage lights, it became apparent that the old painted setting was no longer satisfactory. Furniture painted on the drops or wings became glaringly false when the actors could neither use nor touch it. Painted shadows and painted three-dimensional trim were no longer convincing when the audience viewed them from a much shorter distance. The gaping spaces between the wings became more and more objectionable until that time when some unrecorded genius thought to turn the wings at right angles to the proscenium arch and to join them edge to edge. With the wing-space entrances removed it was necessary to cut door openings into the side wall flats. When this monumental step toward greater reality was accomplished, it was not long before openings for windows and fireplaces came into being. Finally, the old cloth borders that had masked the tops of both wings and drops were replaced by a ceiling piece—and so was born the box setting.

Once three-dimensional form of the setting had been established, steps

---

[3] Nicoll, *op. cit.*, p. 175.

toward greater and greater reality followed in rapid succession. Painted trim was replaced by three-dimensional baseboards, paneling, chair rails, plate rails, picture molding, and cornices. The same sense of authenticity as that found in the architectural features of a setting was sought for the floor coverings, furniture, and decorative trim. Directors and designers had found a new tool and they used it to excess. Settings became more and more elaborate until the actors were all but lost in a maze of details. The constant striving toward greater and greater reality reached its peak in this country with the work of David Belasco (1854–1931). For his production of *The Easiest Way* in 1909, Belasco found a room in a dilapidated rooming house that possessed the exact qualities he sought, even down to wallpaper and furnishings; he had the room dismantled and literally transferred to the stage for his production.[4]

Summary

This capsule survey of the history of scenic design has been used to emphasize two facts. First, it took man literally centuries to arrive at the conclusion that plays were best presented within settings that clearly indicated the period, the country, and the locale in which the action took place. Second, no sooner had man perfected completely realistic staging techniques than he began to revolt against them and to seek other means of expression which he felt were more dynamic and meaningful. The period from 1900 to the present time has been characterized by an extraordinary willingness to experiment with new forms and new techniques in producing a play.

Prior to 1900 standardization in production methods had characterized all the great periods throughout the history of drama. A Greek or a Roman play was produced out-of-doors against the architectural façade of the scene building; medieval drama employed the use of symbols and suggestive set pieces; plays of the Renaissance and those written as late as the middle of the nineteenth century were usually presented against some variation of the two-dimensional drop and wing setting. True, there were minor variations in staging techniques that reflected cultural and geographic differences, but, in general, the staging conventions remained standardized with little thought given to the idea that each play should be designed and set to enhance its individual character.

[4] David Belasco, *The Theatre Through Its Stage Door*, New York, Harper & Row, 1919.

12

STYLES IN
SCENIC DESIGN

At the turn of the century the field of scenic design entered a period of development and experimentation unparalleled by any comparable span of years in twenty-five centuries of play production.

In one respect the period of realism in the theatre was radically different from the other great periods that preceded it. It completely abandoned standardization of production techniques and sought new methods of expression that were reflected in all phases of theatre work. During the twentieth century influences and counterinfluences came with confusing rapidity; playwriting concerned itself with any and all subject matter, expressed in new or old forms; new schools of acting and new theories of direction were formulated; even the form of theatre buildings was questioned and stages of novel plan came into being. It was only natural that in these circumstances scenic design should change as rapidly as the other elements of production and face in new directions. It was obvious that no single style of design could possibly be satisfactory for all types of plays or be used with equal success on all kinds of stages. Designers began to experiment and to express themselves with new forms as they attempted to keep up with the changing patterns of drama. Out of all this experimentation there developed a group of styles, or methods of expression in design, that found favor with directors and audiences and that have been used with enough regularity to be dignified by a name.

Before beginning any discussion of the styles, it is well for the reader to understand several points. There is no exact line of demarcation between any of these styles; while it is possible to design a production within the limitations of any one style, more frequently the designer makes use of two or more styles in combination as he seeks to express the idea of a particular play. Moreover, there is in this field a confusion of terms; several of these styles are known by the same name, and different names are sometimes given by different people to the same style. When someone feels he has found a more descriptive name for a given style, he introduces it and thus adds to the confusion. The whole subject of style in design is so comparatively new and so subject to change that only time is likely to bring any stability to the terminology.

Perhaps it should be mentioned that there is no merit in a study of these styles merely for the sake of being able to identify and catalogue them. Anyone genuinely interested in design will make a thorough study of them because they are important tools of his trade and because he must work with them as knowingly as he does with the elements of composition. Finally, it may be of some help in understanding these styles of design to make clear that they differ one from another only in the degree to which they vary from reality. We start with a complete recording of fact, as in naturalism, and move progressively away from it toward a greater and greater dependence upon imagination. It is on this scale of differentiation that the following discussions are based; the listings are not in chronological order.

Naturalism

Naturalism as a style in design met the same obstacles and objections that Emile Zola and his followers found when they espoused naturalism as a form in dramatic literature. The mere placing of a great number of architectural and physical details on stage did not necessarily result in a good design any more than the observing and recording of facts as they dealt with the life of man resulted in a play. In order to produce a setting that carried a real impact to an audience, it was, and is, essential that the designer exercise his artistic judgment in selecting certain details and discarding others, in rearranging the details in such a way as to give emphasis to important parts of a setting, and in inventing new ways to solve the old problems of sight lines, rapid shifts, etc. In short, a stage setting without imagination can add little to the interpretation of a play.

Naturalism in design is characterized by a meticulous recording of facts and their incorporation into the stage picture. Ideally, this is to be done with such finesse and skill that the setting appears to belong to life itself rather than to the theatre. It is photographic in nature; and like so many photographs, taken with no thought to selectivity of subject matter, it contains material that is at best unnecessary and at worst disturbing or distracting. Besides the aesthetic objections to this style of design, naturalism is subject to several very practical objections: settings are so cumbersome in form and construction and so filled with meaningless details that they become prohibitively expensive; too much time is required to construct them; they cannot be shifted in a permissible length of time and are therefore poorly suited to plays requiring several settings; and perhaps, most important of all, such settings frequently dominate the actors.

NATURALISM

PLATE 58 *Pygmalion,* produced at the University Theatre, State University of Iowa, directed by V. Morton, designed by A. S. Gillette

By 1900 naturalism as a style in literature had run its course, and as a style in design it was used infrequently after 1914, though on rare occasions it can still be seen. Designers of today are indebted to it for two reasons: it focused attention on the importance of authentic details, and it pointed up the need for the designer to find original source material on which to base his designs.

Realism

Of all the styles in design, realism is the easiest for the student to grasp. Whether or not he has had an opportunity to see examples of it on stage is of little consequence; he has been subjected to a constant parade of it in the movies and on television.

The period of realism in playwriting is not a fad of a season or two, but extends over the years beginning with the plays of Chekhov and Ibsen down to the work of Arthur Miller, Tennessee Williams, William Inge, and other moderns. It has been subjected to many modifications and influences, but in spite of all the changes realism has remained the dominant force in playwriting of the twentieth century. Since it is the play itself that sets the pattern for all phases of a production, it is not surprising that scenic design should reflect these variations and modifications while at the same time remaining basically realistic.

The realistic set is based on authentic source material but the details have been carefully selected and some of them exaggerated in size and scale for greater theatrical effectiveness. To all appearances the setting seems complete; it has its full complement of such architectural features as doors, windows, walls, ceiling, and any other details the designer feels may help to establish the proper environment for the play. To the casual observer it may appear as though it were taken from real life. However, a more critical analysis reveals several factors. In order to comply with the sight line demands and with the dimensions imposed by most stages, the size of the setting is increased beyond that of the room on which the design was based. As an example, take a modern kitchen. The average size of such a room is about 12′ × 14′ with a ceiling height of about 8′. On stage the width of the room is extended to 30′ or 32′ (32′ is the average width of a proscenium stage), its depth is near 15′ or 16′ and the height of the walls is increased to approximately 14′. The number and size of the furnishings found in an average kitchen when placed in such an enlarged room would seem lost and out of proportion to the wall areas. One of the designer's problems is the adjustment of line and form to overcome this difficulty. This he may do by breaking up the planes of the walls into interesting shapes, by adjusting window arrangements, and by exaggerating the length and width of such features as worktables, drain boards, and cupboard spaces. There is a fine point beyond which he cannot go in exaggerating dimensions; he must not increase them to such an extent that they become out of scale with the actors who are to use them.

Another point that a casual observer may not detect is that the furnishings of most realistic settings have been carefully selected and are usually confined to those pieces that are actually employed by the actors in the performance of their stage business. One exception to this is found in pieces of furniture or equipment that are included, even if not touched by the actors, because they are so inherently a part of a particular room that their absence would call attention to itself.

There is always a question as to how far a designer or a director can carry his desire for realistic effects without running the risk of having it become a distraction to the play. This is more likely to occur with props and their use than with any other feature of a setting. It is amazing how fascinated an

PLATE 59 *Calvario*, produced at the University Theatre, State University of
Iowa, directed by E. C. Mabie, designed by Lemuel Ayers

Death of a Salesman, produced at the University Theatre, State University of
Iowa, directed by Gregory Foley, designed by A. S. Gillette

audience becomes when it sees real food being cooked or water running from a faucet on stage. In a production of *Juno and the Paycock* the director felt that having two of his actors cook bacon on an old dilapidated stove would be a good bit of stage business. A can of solidified alcohol hidden inside the stove provided the heat; the rest was up to the actors and gave them an opportunity they seemed to relish. A stove lid was noisily removed, the fire started, and a frying pan clattered into place. Slabs of bacon were slapped into the pan and it wasn't long before the unmistakable sizzle of frying bacon could be heard. The progress of its aroma could be followed from front to back of the auditorium as one row after another of the audience sniffed, then whispered knowingly to their neighbors that the actors were really cooking bacon on stage! All interest in what the actors were saying completely disappeared while the audience enjoyed the fragrance of two slices of bacon!

Equally fascinating to an audience is running water, whether it flows from a faucet, rises from a fountain, or falls in the form of rain. At the University of Iowa production of *The Importance of Being Earnest* it was decided to include in the garden scene a fountain with a modest spray of real water. During rehearsals the fountain behaved in a well-ordered fashion, but with the increased use of plumbing facilities when the building was open to the public, there was no controlling the water pressure on the third floor of the building where the theatre was located. The spray of water from the fountain varied from a trickle to squirts that flew above head height and the actors were hopelessly upstaged by the fountain. Under the circumstances more was lost than was gained by the use of real water.

Pictorial Realism

One variation of realism, not seen with any great regularity in the theatre today, is a style called pictorial realism. The term "pictorial" seems to be especially well chosen, for it implies that the emphasis is placed on the compositional qualities of the setting rather than on a faithful depiction of realistic details. Wherever possible the emphasis is placed on impressive color harmonies and on bold use of line, form, and mass. The simplification of detail that usually characterizes such work makes them easily appreciated by those who have made no special study of design. Frequently such designs employ symmetrical balance and an obvious use of motif or pattern; when these characteristics are carefully adjusted, they result in extremely effective space and area relationships. A sense of reality is retained in such designs, but greater importance is given to the elements of composition than to accuracy of realistic details. Perhaps another way of describing pictorial realism would be to say that it is an idealized treatment of realistic backgrounds achieved by simplification of detail and by stressing the compositional manner in which the detail is handled.

PICTORIAL REALISM

PLATE 60 *Caliban, A Shakespearian Interlude Combining Scenes from* The Merchant of Venice, Romeo and Juliet, *and* The Winter's Tale, designed by Robert Edmond Jones

The greatest exponent of this style of design in America was Robert Edmond Jones. A study of his designs will reveal the great economy of detail and the unusual interest lent to each design by his treament of its compositional elements.

Suggestive Realism

A style of design that has found favor with directors, designers, and audiences alike is called suggestive realism. As the name implies, it can be described simply by stating that it allows a part to stand for the whole. It is the simplification of a realistic setting by the elimination of all unnecessary detail. The degree to which a setting can be simplified depends on the nature of the play, the type of locale being treated, and the extent to which actors have practical business related to the set itself.

It is possible to treat a suggestive setting in a great variety of ways. They may range all the way from a setting that at first glance seems almost complete in its details to one that has been reduced to one architectural feature and a few props. A setting might retain most of its wall surfaces but have the ceiling and the upper sections of the walls removed, creating an interesting omission line that is emphasized by the background against which the setting is placed. Or the walls may be reduced to nothing more than sections extending below the chair rails with doors and windows indicated by skeleton frames. The elimination of detail may be carried still farther. In the setting for the blacksmith shop in a production of *The Patriots,* nothing remained but the forge, the anvil, and a partial beaming of one of the horse stalls; the rest of the stage was lost in darkness. The log cabin in a production of *Abe Lincoln in Illinois* was reduced still farther; it consisted of a fireplace, a stool, a table, and a single candle.

SUGGESTIVE REALISM
PLATE 61   *La Traviata,* produced at McBride Hall, State University of Iowa,
directed by H. Shiffler, designed by A. S. Gillette

This style of design is known by a variety of names. But whether it is called social, simplified, or conditional realism; fragmentary, minimized, contour, or profile scenery, or whether it is simply called impressionism, it possesses qualities that have made it a continuing favorite with producing groups.

Directors have found it to be a style that is adaptable to a wide variety of plays, dramatically expressive, and economical for plays that require several settings. It can also be applied to styles of design other than realism, that is, it is possible to have suggestive stylized scenery or suggestive scenery that is formal or expressionistic in nature.

Designers find suggestive realism both a flexible and a challenging style in which to work. The effectiveness of a design done in this manner is directly proportional to how well the designer has selected the focal or dominant object and to how well he has treated it in respect to the elements of composition. The elimination of all unnecessary details from the setting forces the designer to put greater reliance on imagination, arrangement, and pure design in the handling of the few features he retains. The style is adaptable for theatres with limited stage facilities, small crews, and limited time schedules, since the scenery requires little space on stage and in storage, it requires fewer stage hands to shift it, and it obviously requires less time to construct than a complete setting.

Audiences find this type of scenery interesting and refreshing. While it provides them with a visual background that hints at a particular locale, it allows them to create out of their own experience and imagination any detail that their eyes tell them is lacking.

Problems of a special nature are encountered when working with suggestive realism. These problems, though sometimes associated with other styles as well, occur with such frequency that some mention of them should be made. The best way to avoid trouble is to be aware of the possible sources of trouble.

It should be quite apparent that not all source material on which the designer must base his designs lends itself with the same degree of success to a suggestive treatment. For example, it is easier to simplify and suggest architectural features than objects taken directly from nature. Man-made structures, whether part of an interior or an exterior view, usually possess some distinctive feature that can be selected to serve as a focal point for a design. Finding the focal point or a distinctive feature in a forest, a mountain range, or a wheat field is a little more difficult. However, even this can be done by extreme simplification and by the very careful use of lighting effects. In a production of *The Crucible* at the State University of Iowa, the forest scene was reduced to two trees—one was standing with its gnarled branches disappearing into the darkness above; the other had fallen, leaving its stump and rotting trunk near the base of the first. The mountains in *Distant Drums* were suggested by three large boulders on and around which the actors could move. The wheat field called for in an original script was suggested by a corner of the field, represented by two sections of a fence that met at an angle and by a dilapidated two-wheeled seeder left standing in the field.

Another source of trouble is the difficulty in maintaining the same type of treatment for all the designs used for a multiset production. Elmer Rice's *Dream Girl* has seventeen scenes in the first act and thirteen in the second. The scenes follow one another in rapid order, and while there is some duplication of settings, each scene differs in locale from the preceding scene. Any great dissimilarity in style between scenes becomes apparent very quickly under such conditions. Every possible effort should be made to have all the designs appear unified, as integral parts of a single idea. This is usually accomplished by giving each setting something in common with all others. This may be a similar treatment of line, of color, or of form. In addition to what the artist may do with design itself in his treatment of subject matter, he may resort to other devices in an effort to give a sense of unity to the visual aspects of a production. A false proscenium which is distinctive in form and especially related to the nature of the play provides a strong unifying force for settings seen through its opening. Equally successful is the use of projections thrown upon a cyclorama or drop to form a related background for the designs. However, extreme care must be exercised in the use of such projections to prevent their dominating both the acting areas and the settings. This is usually a matter of controlling the intensity of the light and of making certain that the design of the projections is unobtrusive in form. A distinctive acting area arrangement, possibly consisting of steps, levels, or ramps, on which the suggestive settings can be placed has also been used with success as a device for unifying a multi-scened production.

The suggestive realistic setting requires that special attention be paid to lighting if the design is to achieve its maximum effectiveness. Frequently a setting occupies only a part of the stage, and the scene shifts are made in blackouts or with one scene fading out as another fades in. Both schemes presuppose a sensitive control board well handled and accurately cued, as well as an adequate supply of lighting instruments properly mounted and focused. Specific lighting, which isolates comparatively small areas of the stage, is used much more extensively than general illumination in such productions. Lighting must be carefully planned and carefully synchronized with the action and scene shifts.

The designer using suggestive realism must give special attention to two aspects of a production that normally present him with but minimal problems—masking and bracing. In consultation with the director, decisions must be made on whether the actors approach and leave the entrances in darkness or whether the entrances and exits are masked by background draperies carefully arranged for this purpose. The designer must be especially careful in determining the height of all units of scenery. Otherwise, he may create an unintentionally comic effect by having a unit that masks all but the bobbing head of an actor as he walks on or off stage behind it. When actors are to be seen over the top of scenery there should never be any doubt left in the minds of the spectators that it is intentional. When it is apparent by the very nature of the design that complete masking is impossible and obviously not intended, no distraction is caused by the lack of it, but an audience is quick to detect the sneaking figure of an actor trying to conceal himself behind inadequate masking.

The designer cannot ignore the special problems that bracing presents with the use of this type of scenery. Since he frequently makes use of isolated units of scenery, the designer may be deprived of many of the devices normally used in bracing because they can be seen by the audience. He may rearrange the design to permit conventional bracing;

he may use devices such as modified rigid or folding jacks, sockets, foot-irons, and guy wire; or he may anchor the scenery solidly to rolling wagons. There are few effects on stage quite so devastating to the peace of mind of an audience as a teetering unit of scenery that appears always on the verge of falling.

Stylization

Another style in scenic design, one that has made a permanent place for itself in the theatre because of its adaptability and distinctive qualities, is known by the confusing name of stylization. It is confusing because, although stylization is just as distinctive a style as naturalism, realism, pictorial realism, and suggestive realism, the term stylization is not descriptive. It is odd that no one has suggested a name that is really indicative of the qualities of this style, but such is the case.

Stylization is familiar to us all; we have been exposed to it in various forms from the time we first enjoyed the illustrations in children's picture books. We saw it again in the funny papers, in comic books, and we have seen excellent examples of it in animated movies and in some television commercials. Basically, it can be described as the amusing telling of a story by graphic means. It invariably employs an exaggeration of color, line, and mass in the treatment of objects taken from life. The designer has adapted and arranged his source material to conform to a particular style of expression rather than to a faithful recording of its appearance in nature.

A well-executed stylized design invariably has two characteristics. First, the source on which the design is based remains true to its natural form and remains recognizable for what it is. Second, the material is treated in an exaggerated manner that is sometimes original, often unexpected, and sometimes amusing. There are several approaches the designer may take in developing a style of expression; some of the techniques commonly used for that purpose are listed below.

Color. An unexpected color may be substituted for the natural color of an object. A delightful musical skit seen on a London stage used this idea effectively. The scene was an exterior in Scotland representing a woodland glade flanked by bushes and trees on either side and including a distant view of mountains. The forms of the bushes and trees, the foliage overhead, and the distant mountains were all realistically treated in silhouette, but instead of being painted colors one would normally expect, they were painted plaid.

Line. Realistic forms may be simplified through the use of line alone (line is used here to mean the boundary separating one color mass or area from another and also the outline that describes the shape of realistic forms). By simplifying the descriptive shape of objects Walt Disney has developed his distinctive style. There is absolutely no mistaking the true nature of

STYLIZATION

PLATE 62 *Mrs. McThing*, produced at the University Theatre, State University
of Iowa, directed by Willard Welsh, designed by Richard Knaub

The Country Wife, produced at the University Theatre, State University of Iowa, directed by David Knauf, designed by John Kasarda

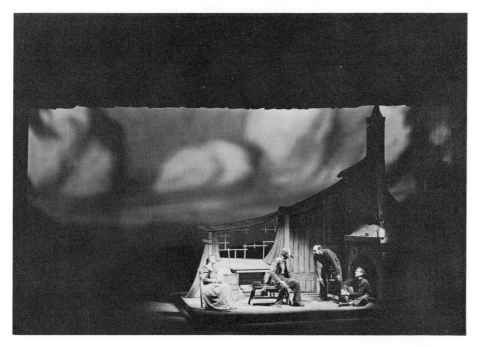

Fragmentary stylization. *Dark of the Moon*, first produced at the University Theatre, State University of Iowa, as *Barbara Allen*, directed by Hunton Sellman, designed by John Boydt

Ondine, produced at the University Theatre, State University of Iowa, directed by Willard Welsh, designed by A. S. Gillette

The Doctor in Spite of Himself, produced at the University Theatre, State University of Iowa, directed by H. Shiffler, designed by Andrew Loshbough

what he has drawn; the objects are readily identifiable with what they represent. Yet, the deft manner in which he simplifies their shapes gives them their distinctive and amusing qualities.

Mass.   The exaggeration of mass (those areas occupied on stage by three-dimensional units of scenery) is another method whereby the artist can give a specialized quality to his design. This he may do by changing normally vertical or horizontal lines of architectural structures into lines placed at odd angles. The designs by Akimov for the production of *My Crime* at the Comedy Theatre in Leningrad utilized this approach perfectly (see Plate 73). The first scene depicted a view of an artist's top floor studio and the adjoining rooftops of Paris. The vertical lines of all the buildings toed in at the top; even the floor of the studio and the encircling balcony sloped downward toward the curtain line. This gave the setting an unreal quality that was perfectly in keeping with the farcical nature of the play.

Perspective.   Altering the principles of perspective to produce an unusual effect is a technique used repeatedly in stylization. The horizon line may be raised to an unreasonable height which produces the effect of looking down upon the setting, rather than into it. The vanishing points may be placed in unusual positions or several vanishing points may be used in drawing an object usually controlled by one. Dwarfing the size of the human figure or enlarging it to giant proportions can be accomplished by adjusting the scale of the faked or forced perspective. This last principle was used to good effect in two productions given at the State University of Iowa. In *Alice in Wonderland* the scenery, towering above the figure of Alice, made her appear tiny by comparison; just the reverse was true in the play *Paul and the Blue Ox*—Paul dwarfed everything around him.

Materials.   The unexpected use of objects or materials customarily used for another specific purpose can result in an amusing and whimsical effect. The walls of two settings in *The School for Taxpayers*, designed by Tischler and produced at the Zavadski Theatre in Moscow, were formed by wicker clothes baskets supported by a pipe framework (see Plate 77). This scenery was just as improbable and as delightful as the play and provided a perfect visual accompaniment for it.

SUMMARY

The artist may get the idea for his decorative scheme from any number of sources. It may be based on some characteristic quality of the play and its subject matter. The period of the play may provide the inspiration, or it may be found in some distinctive trait of the country where the action is laid. No matter what the source for the designer's inspiration, it is usually executed through one or more of the techniques just mentioned. In addition to this, the artist always hopes to leave on his designs the imprint of his own individual manner of working. The qualities which distinguish

FORMALISM

PLATE 63 Formalism combined with suggestive realistic fragments. *Caprices of Marianne*, produced at the University Theatre, State University of Iowa, directed by Philip Benson, designed by A. S. Gillette

Hamlet, produced at the University Theatre, State University of Iowa, directed by Lael Woodbury, designed by A. S. Gillette

his work from that of other designers are apt to be more apparent in a stylized design than in any other kind.

One of the advantages of working with stylization is its adaptability to a wide range of plays. As a general rule, if the play is not tragic or overly realistic in nature, if it does not require deep concentration to follow the ramifications of the plot, the use of stylization can be considered. It is difficult to design a children's story or a fairy tale without resorting to stylized design. Here the exaggerated, intriguing qualities of stylization seem to be at their best. It is equally appropriate for fantasies, dance dramas, ballet, and operettas. Certain types of satirical plays like *The Importance of Being Earnest* are frequently handled in this manner. Plays of a highly imaginative nature and those revolving about dream sequences can often be most effectively designed by using stylization.

There are, however, two faults frequently encountered in productions where stylization has been employed. It can be, and too often is, imposed on a play for which it is not suited. At other times, the designer simply becomes so intrigued with carrying out an idea that he fails to consider the other elements of production. Close collaboration between the director and the designer can avoid the first of these faults, but, in spite of their most careful efforts, they may not quite visualize the effect that the designs will have on the actors, the costumes, or the lighting. When working in this style, it is more than ever important for the designer to confer conscientiously and regularly with the costumer and the lighting director.

Formalism

Moving still farther away from reality is another style called formalism. This is the complete antithesis of everything the designer seeks to incorporate into a realistic design. He now seeks to create a setting that is neither pictorial nor representational of any period, country, or locale. The emphasis in formalism is placed on conventionalizing the forms used in a stage setting and on creating an interesting arrangement of playing spaces that are in no way indicative of natural objects or a particular place. The goal of the formalists originally was to return to a completely functional theatre, a permanent architectural background neutral enough in its features and arrangement to allow the presentation of all types of plays.

Since the turn of the century there have been any number of experiments carried out along the general lines recommended by the formalists. Out of these have grown a series of production techniques that have succeeded in accomplishing some of the goals set by the formalists. Some of the derivatives of formalism should be examined briefly.

DRAPERY SETTINGS

Theatres with conventional proscenium arches have been adapted to formalism by the substitution of drapery backgrounds for scenery. The

DRAPERY SETTING

PLATE 64 *The Doctor's Dilemma*, produced at the University Theatre, State University of Iowa, directed by James Clancy, designed by A. S. Gillette

intention is to create a background that is completely neutral, noncommital, and self-effacing. Draperies used for this purpose are generally very dark or black in color. They are hung as far from the acting area as circumstances will permit, and every effort is made to keep the stage lights from striking them. If this is successfully achieved, the stage appears to be a void. Actors, properties, and forms stand out in striking relief against such a background.

SPACE STAGES

The space stage is closely related to the drapery setting in its total effect. It may have a background formed by draperies or by an enclosing cyclorama. Frequently, however, the acting areas are occupied by interesting platform and stair arrangements that give the director an opportunity to add variety and picturization to the movements of his actors. Specific lighting is used extensively to pick out and isolate different acting areas while the remainder of the stage is lost in darkness.

ARENA STAGES

A typical arena stage may be described as an acting area completely encircled by an audience. This arrangement holds the use of scenery to an absolute minimum since anything higher than a foot or two is likely to interfere with the audience's view of the acting area. This type of theatre fulfills the formalists' goals of suppressing scenery and of throwing the full focus of attention on the play and the acting. The amount of furniture is often restricted to those pieces required by the stage business and even these few pieces of furniture may be replaced by cubes and rectangular blocks. It is true that not all arena productions are handled in this stripped-down style. In an effort to relieve the monotony of repeated arena-style productions, some theatres increasingly resort to the use of whatever suggestive scenery the designer can contribute without interfering with sight lines. By the use of low set pieces, platforms, steps, and furniture it is possible to arrange a setting that is suggestive in form and effective in use. However, when this is done, a production loses whatever claim it might have had toward fulfilling the formalists' goal of being neither suggestive nor representational of a particular place; certainly it loses many of the advantages inherent in this style. These advantages are obvious. Almost any room large enough to house an audience and an acting area can be utilized as a theatre and without the heavy cost associated with backstage equipment and its maintenance. Most of the time and work normally spent on scenery can be eliminated and the cost of production reduced proportionally.

SPACE STAGE

PLATE 65 *Othello,* produced at the University Theatre, State University of Iowa, directed by H. Shiffler, designed by Keith Michaels

ARENA STAGE

PLATE 66   *Trespassers*, produced at the Studio Theatre, State University of Iowa,
directed by Philip Benson, designed by A. S. Gillette

UNIT SETTINGS

Variety in the form of unit settings is as diversified as the imaginations
of the designers who conceive them, so it is difficult to give a description
that does justice to them all. But, in general, the unit set can be said to
consist of a permanent structure, capable of some alteration in form, that
is usually supplemented by a series of screens, plugs, platforms, and stair
units that may be arranged to meet the needs of a particular play. Such a
setting may be looked upon as a piece of flexible stage equipment; it belongs
to the stage rather than the play. In this sense it complies with the true
purpose of the formalists' theory.

The Studio Theatre at the State University of Iowa is equipped with
such a unit setting. Over the past six years this setting has been adapted
for a variety of plays that includes *The Good Woman of Setzuan*, *Danton's
Death*, *A Month in the Country*, *Cyclops*, *The Miracle Worker*, and *King
of the Dark Chamber*. Judging by the attendance of a paying public at these
and many other productions, the audiences have had no objections to seeing
the same basic setting used as a background for many plays.

The Studio Theatre at Iowa came into being because the department
felt the need of supplying students in playwriting, acting, and directing

with a laboratory restricted to their use. Used both as a classroom and for public performances it provides other outlets for student activities to supplement those offered by the regular productions scheduled at the University Theatre. This literally meant sponsoring a dual program. Because of budgetary limitations and the students' lack of time for additional heavy crew assignments, it was apparent from the beginning that whatever settings were used had to be functional in nature. One end of an unused gymnasium provided the building for our Studio Theatre. A 6' wide run-

UNIT SETTING

PLATE 67   Model of the unit set used at the Studio Theatre, State University of
Iowa, designed by A. S. Gillette

ning track suspended 11' from the floor circled the walls of the gym. A second-level acting area was created at one end of the room by adding an 8' × 24' extension to the running track. Both the track and the new extension are suspended from overhead beams leaving the area below free of supporting columns. Access to this second level is provided by two portable stairways, each consisting of two stairway units and a landing. These can be used in any position or used in combination if desired. Twenty-four parallels, each 4' × 8' × 1'-2", can be arranged in any shape to form the lower acting area. These can be extended back under the second-story acting level to form the equivalent of an "inner below." A draw curtain suspended from the underside of the upper level can be closed to mask the inner below when it is not needed. Many step units with varying numbers of steps but all with 7″ risers can be used in conjunction with the parallels. A series of two-fold and three-fold flats of varying heights and widths provide necessary masking and may be used anywhere on stage. Black masking draperies, hung from the hand rails of the old running track, form corridors to conceal from the audience the movement of actors and crews. An audience of 200 can be accommodated in the auditorium which, like the setting, can be rearranged. Chairs (the same ones used when the room serves as a classroom) may be placed in a single bank facing the stage or divided to enclose the acting area on two, three, or four sides. Some of the chairs are placed in rows on the floor level, others on platforms for better sight lines. A large scaled model of the setting is used by directors and designers in determining what arrangement will best meet the needs of their play.

ARCHITECTURAL STAGES

The term "architectural stage," whether applied to outdoor stages or to stages enclosed within a theatre, describes them well. These stages may be patterned after the Greek or Elizabethan stage or they may be entirely new in concept. In either case they are usually permanent structures, perhaps incorporating several acting levels, and intended to serve as a neutral background for plays of all types.

Sheldon Cheney, in discussing stages of this type, has the following to say about them: "The first reason for this type of theatre, however, is that the audiences, if the director's non-realistic intent is made clear through the frank formalism of the playing space, will accept the convention of one stage remaining throughout the many scenes of a play, throughout many plays; that a declared platform for acting, obviously without means for changing its own character, without facilities for picturing many places in nature, will not be expected by the audience so to change, or to give back a view of natural surroundings. Instead the imagination of the spectator will supply new backgrounds insofar as needed." [1]

That so many of the newer architectural stages owe their inspiration to the Elizabethan stage is not surprising. There are those who feel that man has never devised a more flexible stage nor one better suited to the staging of multiscened plays than the stage on which it is generally concluded that Shakespeare's plays were produced. This permanent structure was divided into a forestage, middle stage, inner below, inner above, and a balcony as separate acting areas; access to each was given from conveniently placed doorways. As a scene progressed, the unused acting areas could be preset with props and furnishings and later revealed with no more delay than the opening of a curtain. Under such circumstances the play's action could move from scene to scene as rapidly as the director wished.

Modern variations in the forms of architectural stages are many, and

[1] Sheldon Cheney, *Stage Decoration*, New York, John Day, 1928, chap. XII, pp. 113–114.

usually with each variation the director and designer have sought new production techniques that allow them to capitalize on the form of their new stages without sacrificing the special quality that makes a setting expressive of and suitable for a particular play. Two notable variations of the architectural stage, known to many American theatre-goers, are the Tyrone Guthrie Theatre at Minneapolis and the Shakespeare Festival Theatre at Stratford, Ontario. It is not surprising that there is a marked similarity between the two since the guiding hands of Tyrone Guthrie and Tanya Moiseiwitsch were involved in both enterprises. Each theatre has an open stage with no proscenium arch or front curtain, but with an acting platform of asymmetrical design. This stage "thrusts" out into the auditorium and the audience faces the stage from three sides. This arrangement brings the spectators closer to the acting area than is possible in a theatre with a conventional proscenium stage. In back of the acting platforms are the architectural façades. At the Guthrie Theatre in Minneapolis this façade consists of an irregularly shaped wall divided into two large sections. Each section is formed by three panels pierced by smaller sections that can be removed to form openings or doorways. These large sections can be rolled to either side of the stage during act intermissions; this permits rolling platforms to pass from backstage to their playing positions on the acting area. When the action of the play so dictates, a second-level acting area can be incorporated into the basic rolling platforms. Such was the case in the production of *The Caucasian Chalk Circle* produced during their 1965 season.

The stage of the Shakespeare Festival Theatre at Stratford, Ontario, was designed by Tanya Moiseiwitsch in 1953 in collaboration with Tyrone Guthrie. The plans were slightly altered in 1957 when the permanent theatre was built to replace their famous tent theatre. In the fall of 1961 Miss Moiseiwitsch and Brian Jackson redesigned parts of the stage to improve sight lines and to overcome certain technical difficulties. The photograph in Plate 68 shows the stage as it appears today. The architectural façade of the stage has a permanent second-level acting area, much like a balcony, that is supported by five columns. The columns rest on a raised section of the hexagonally shaped main stage which thrusts out into the auditorium. The audience faces the stage from three sides. The area beneath the balcony houses the main entrance to the stage. Directly above it and providing access to the balcony is a second central entrance. Stairways descend from the balcony on either side to landings that service doorways placed at the extreme sides of the stage. From these landings a second run of stairs leads back to the main stage. Counting the two tunnels approaching the stage from beneath the auditorium, the apron trap door, and the auditorium aisles there are sixteen entrances to the stage.[2]

The same philosophy of production has been followed by the Tyrone Guthrie and the Shakespeare Festival theatres. Emphasis on scenic spectacle

[2] I am indebted to the management of both the Tyrone Guthrie Theatre and the Shakespeare Festival Theatre for the photographs and descriptive material.

ARCHITECTURAL STAGE
PLATE 68   The Tyrone Guthrie Theatre, Minneapolis

The Tyrone Guthrie Theatre, Minneapolis; photograph taken during a performance of *The Three Sisters*

has been held to a minimum while attention has been largely directed toward splendidly designed and constructed costumes and meticulously executed properties. This is not meant to imply that the use of all scenery must be abandoned on stages of this type. If a director feels that a particular play will benefit from the use of scenery in some form, it is quite possible to give it to him. That such scenery can be used effectively without conflicting with the basic architectural stage has been convincingly proved.

The Stratford Festival Theatre, Stratford, Ontario (Peter Smith, photographer)

It is interesting to note that present-day theatres with architectural stages bear a remarkably close resemblance to early Greek and Elizabethan theatres. Each has an acting area surrounded on three sides by an audience; each possesses an architectural façade adjacent to the acting platform; and each is intended to be used with a minimum of scenery. The one really outstanding difference is that the theatres of today are enclosed. Viewed in this light, modern theatre in its physical aspects could almost be said to have come full circle from its earliest recorded beginnings and to be now again at the point from which it started.

EXPRESSIONISM

Near the end of the nineteenth century a new style in playwriting initiated still another and more violent revolt against realism; it is called expressionism. August Strindberg is usually credited with laying the foundation for work in this medium with such plays as *Miss Julie*, *The Dream Play*, and *The Spook Sonata*. Expressionism reached the height of its popularity in Germany with the work of Georg Kaiser and Ernst Toller, but soon it began to decline in favor and its influence ceased to be as great after the middle 1920s. Expressionism gained only a few followers in the United States. Elmer Rice's *The Adding Machine*, Eugene O'Neill's *The Great God Brown*, *The Hairy Ape*, and George S. Kaufman and Marc Connelly's *Beggar on Horseback* are examples of American plays whose authors were influenced by the expressionistic movement.

As a movement in writing the term expressionism is indicative of its goal. Playwrights of this school sought to express their ideas of truth in terms of a personal vision of life. They were not at all concerned with recording facts but with "expressing" what man sensed and felt. As a dramatist the expressionist was faced with the formidable task of conveying man's inner thoughts and feelings in dramatic terms that could be understood and appreciated by an audience.

The designer, in his efforts to provide a background for an expressionistic play, is forced away from any reference to recorded fact; he must rely on imagination and attempt to convey by whatever means at his disposal the same expression of truth as that employed by the dramatist. This brings the designer to an impasse; how can he express a human emotion by visual means? Deprived of conventional source material and recorded fact, the designer has usually resorted to distortion or to abstraction. An abstraction used as a scenic background may well hold the attention of an audience simply because it is an interesting composition, but there is grave doubt that the meaning read into it is even close to the intended meaning. Since man is forever attempting to translate the unfamiliar into terms of his own experiences and associations, it is only natural that an abstract design is generally distracting when used as a scenic background. In their efforts to gather meaning from something the truth of which is not readily apparent to them, members of an audience focus their attention on the background rather than on the play and the actors.

The expressionist designer, finding that his ideas are difficult to express through scenery alone, almost invariably makes extensive use of colored light, music, and rhythm. The nebulous quality of projected light, the eerie effect obtained when one projection is superimposed on another or when the two are cross-faded, creates a visual image much more in keeping with the quality of an expressionistic play than can be obtained with two- or three-dimensional scenery no matter how the designer has arranged it. At the State University of Iowa a production of Strindberg's *The Dream Play*, directed by Philip Benson and designed by Thaddeus Thorp, made extensive use of projections. With the exception of two movable platforms and a series of translucent scrim-covered ground rows, the stage was bare

PLATE 69 *The Dream Play*, produced at the University Theatre, State University of Iowa, directed by Philip Benson, designed by Thaddeus Thorp

of all scenery. The projections were thrown on a U-shaped cyclorama that enclosed the acting area on the sides and the back. Each scene was accompanied by a projection that suggested by its color and design something of the same quality found in the script. There was no break in the continuity of the images appearing on the cyclorama—one scene simply melted into the next by the cross-fading of two projections. The moment of fusion that resulted when the two images were superimposed created a design different in form and color from the two projections from which it was obtained. There may have been no unanimity of opinion in the audience as to what the projections meant, but there was no denying their dreamlike vagueness or their effectiveness.

Music and rhythm have long been recognized as effective assets in heightening and reinforcing dramatic action. They have been used to great advantage in plays of all types, but they are especially effective with expressionistic plays. The hypnotic beat of the drums in Eugene O'Neill's *The Emperor Jones* wakens an echoing beat in the feelings of an audience; the accompanying musical score of Paul Green's *Tread the Green Grass* adds to the sympathy an audience feels for Tina's plight; and the score is a dynamic and integral part in Igor Stravinsky's dance-drama *The Tale of a Soldier*.

The expressionist, seeking every means possible to convey his ideas, places great dependence on both auditory and visual production techniques. In fairness to any evaluation of an expressionistic production it should be pointed out that any photographic record of it can illustrate only the visual aspects of it. The style and treatment may be clearly evident from the pictures but the total emotional impact can be judged only when these are seen in conjunction with the auditory effects.

CONSTRUCTIVISM

Constructivism, like expressionism, did not find great favor with the American theatre-going public. The stronghold of this movement was found in Russia in the productions of Vsevelod Meyerhold and Alexander Tairov. Constructivism is identified as an outgrowth of formalism, for its adherents held many of the same views. They felt that the setting should belong to the stage rather than to the play, that there was no need for a setting to suggest the period, country, or locale, and they were strenuously opposed to anything that was reminiscent of earlier realistic staging conventions. Their structures, like those of the formalists, were to stand on stage without benefit of a front curtain and were to remain unchanged from the play's beginning to its end. They differed from the original formalists in their desire to strip from the setting anything that was essentially decorative in nature. They also stressed the elimination of all features that were not absolutely functional and specifically needed for stage business.

CONSTRUCTIVISM

PLATE 70 *The Duchess of Malfi*, produced at the University Theatre, State University of Iowa, directed by Lael Woodbury, designed by A. S. Gillette. The setting, mounted on a revolving stage, is turned in view of the audience to present different playing areas.

The constructivistic setting may be described as a set composed of bare structural or mechanical forms essential to the business of a play and arranged in a manner that will permit an uninterrupted flow of action. The appearance of the setting may closely resemble the effect a director and his stage manager create on stage during early blocking rehearsals when they arrange odds and ends just to "have something to work with." Platforms and parallels are piled one on top of another, spaces between them are bridged by planks, boundary limits are suggested by a ladder on edge or by a plank supported on the backs of two chairs. A stepladder atop a table becomes a second story window, and an imaginative assortment of boxes, planks, stools, folding chairs, or anything else that is serviceable and handy becomes furniture. Oddly enough there is an appeal about such an ingenious arrangement. Though there is little chance of its ever being an aesthetic triumph, it is intriguing if for no other reason than the fun of trying to decide what it is supposed to represent and how it will be used.

Theodore Komisarjevsky, in writing about constructivism, mentions an interesting fact concerning the origin of this style. He states that constructivistic settings began to be used by workers' organizations in Russia after the revolution in 1917. With great insight and well-founded conjecture, it seems to the author, Komisarjevsky states that the style owed its origin as much to a shortage of theatrical building materials as to the wish of producers to avoid the opulent trappings of old bourgeois productions.[3]

[3] Theodore Komisarjevsky, *Settings and Costumes of the Modern Stage*, New York, Studio Publications, 1933, p. 14.

13

EUROPEAN SCENIC DESIGN

The designs chosen for discussion in this chapter were selected for two reasons: to show what can be done when the designer pits his imagination and ingenuity against the limitations of space and equipment and to show how originality and simplicity can be utilized to create distinctive work when the designer is fortunate enough to be working in a well-equipped theatre. This is not a record of current European scene design; some of these plays had been in repertory twelve or fourteen years when I saw them in the mid-1930s. However, they remain the best examples I've found of the traits just mentioned, and it would, I think, be a mistake not to include them here.

All of these productions were the happy products of the Russian repertory theatre system. The advantages of the system were numerous; each theatre had its own building, a permanent business staff, a permanent production staff, and a permanent group of actors—many of whom had worked together for years. Each theatrical organization was subsidized in part by the state, but, what is more important, they operated on the repertory system. This meant that their outstanding productions could be kept in repertory over the years. The sense of cohesion and unity evoked by a group of actors, directors, designers, and technicians working together over a period of years lent to their productions a balance and finish rarely found in other kinds of theatres.

The words "state subsidized theatre" seem to imply spacious, elaborately equipped theatres, but in Russia this was not necessarily the case. True, the Soviet Union has many fine, well-equipped theatres. However, some of the most interesting productions seen there were presented in theatres that had formerly been a garage, a recital hall, an old basement restaurant, a burlesque house, and the basement area under an apartment house. The ingenuity displayed by the designers in overcoming their limitations of space and equipment and the willingness of the theatre staffs to undertake the mounting of multiset plays under such conditions made these productions doubly exciting.

Before any one protests the fact that these productions are not illustrated by photographs, it should be stated that photographs that served my purposes were simply not available. While the theatre management was more than willing to give me what production pictures they had, they were not suited to my use for they were generally pictures taken for publicity purposes. They were excellent close-up shots of the actors, but showed very little of the settings. Had I been permitted to take a camera into a performance, which I wasn't, any pictures I took would probably, for technical reasons, have been valueless anyway. I needed an accurate record of the settings I'd seen and, of necessity, resorted to sketches made during performances. Since drawing in a dark auditorium lent certain mystifying qualities to a sketch, I used the intermissions to add explanatory notes and corrections to the sketches thus made. Late each night, while the details of the production were still fresh in my mind, I reworked each sketch. The drawings accompanying the discussions here were redrawn from those sketches and notes.

Othello

The temporary headquarters of the Radlov Theatre in Leningrad were in an old building that had previously been a garage. It was a very small theatre with an audience capacity of 257. The stage area was an odd shape because the rear wall of the stage house paralleled an outside alleyway rather than the proscenium arch. This arrangement noticeably reduced the amount of backstage space on stage left.

Shakespeare's *Othello* had been directed by Radlov and given an extremely practical, well-executed setting by the designer Basov. The setting included a permanent triple archway that occupied the downstage area. The two side arches provided what amounted to two proscenium doorways, and through the large central archway were seen various arrangements of a permanent setting. A curtain, just upstage of the central archway, could be drawn to provide a forestage area. This allowed the scenery to be shifted in back of the curtain while the acting continued on the forestage.

The permanent setting consisted mainly of several archways and sectional balustrades which could be rearranged quickly into many radically

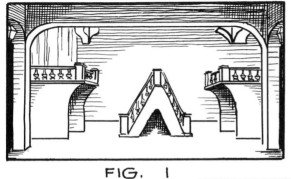

FIG. 1

FIG. 2

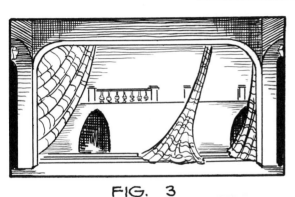

FIG. 3

FIG. 4

FIG. 5

PLATE 71 *Othello*, produced at the Radlov Theatre, Leningrad, directed by Radlov, designed by Basov

different compositions to provide great variety in acting areas and levels. It will be noticed that the arcade was formed by sections which could be separated or joined as needed (see Plate 71, Fig. 2); and, since each section was mounted on casters, they could be reversed to form an unbroken section of wall. The stairways used in Figs. 1 and 2 were repositioned in Figs. 4 and 5 to provide access to the second-level acting areas.

The whole structure, including the permanent triple archway, was covered with plywood rather than with canvas and was stained a rich, reddish brown. The flatness of this covering material was relieved by small, irregularly shaped pieces of plywood stained the same color and applied in a random pattern over the base covering. The shadows cast by side lighting this three-dimensional pattern created an extremely rich textural surface.

Tom Sawyer

At the State Theatre for Young Spectators in Leningrad a production of *Tom Sawyer* was, for me, one of the most exciting and imaginative productions it has ever been my good fortune to see. The State Theatre for Young Spectators is basically a children's theatre, but the only children present were those in the audience; there were none associated with the production. The acting, and it was excellent, was done by adults.

The theatre was housed in a spacious room that had originally been used as a lecture and recital hall in a select school for young ladies. The only access to it, for audience and actors alike, was through double doors, on either side of the room, located near the junction of the side walls with what would normally have been the proscenium wall. There was no stage as such except for a semicircular niche that had a radius of perhaps 10′ and was located in the center of this wall. Across the face of the niche were two sets of oyster gray draw curtains, one above the other. A small free-standing balcony projected between the sets of curtains into the auditorium a distance of 3′ or 4′ and was connected to the platforms below by a ladder. When the curtains above or below the balcony were drawn, they revealed small acting areas similar to the inner above and inner below of a Shake-spearean stage. The remainder of the setting, consisting of platforms of different shapes and levels, extended beyond the curtain line into the auditorium.

The plank-covered, steeply tiered cement rows of seats were semi-circular in shape and can best be compared to the seating arrangement of a small Greco-Roman theatre. They surrounded the platform acting area on three sides. At the back of the auditorium were the lighting control room and an area set aside for the turntables and speakers used for sound effects.

The production had been directed by A. A. Briantzev and the settings created by the designer M. A. Grigoriev. The settings, with the possible exception of the arrangement used for the graveyard, were strictly formal in style; they were neither suggestive nor representational of any specific

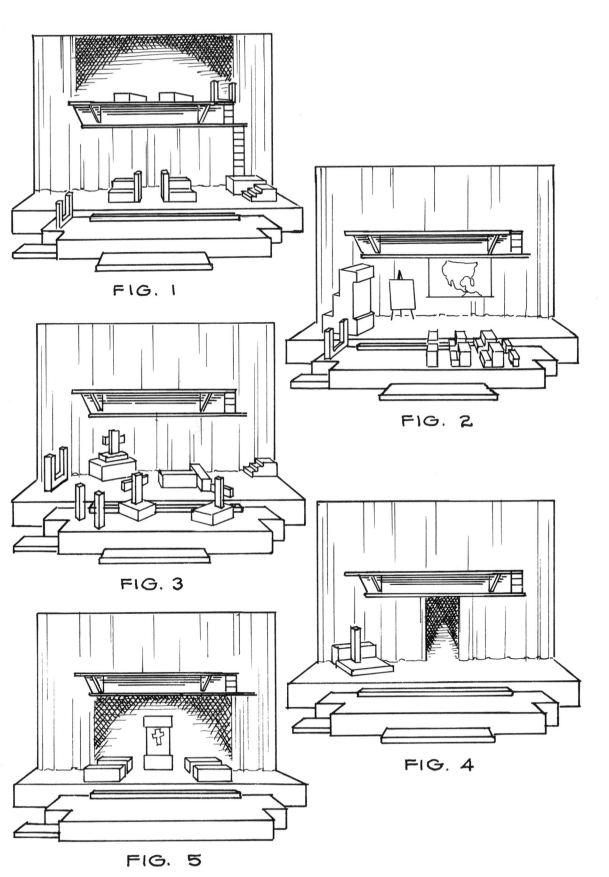

FIG. 1

FIG. 2

FIG. 3

FIG. 4

FIG. 5

PLATE 72 *Tom Sawyer*, produced at the State Theatre for Young Spectators, Leningrad, directed by A. A. Briantzev, designed by M. A. Grigoriev

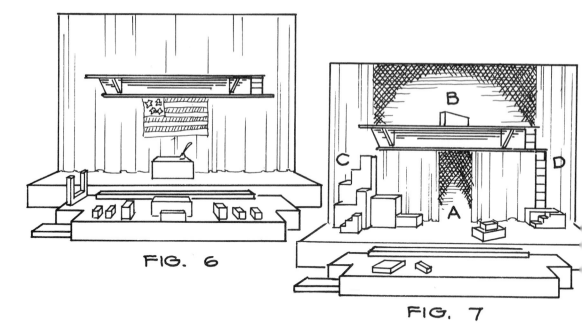

FIG. 6

FIG. 7

locality. Yet, as the different elements of the settings were used by the actors under the imaginative direction of Briantzev, they took on great meaning and became deeply satisfying as the audience supplied the missing details from their own imaginations.

Every part of the setting was painted a bright orange which removed it farther from any likeness to reality. More than anything else the setting resembled a set of children's oversized building blocks that could be rearranged quickly to meet the needs of the following scene. The actors accomplished the changes by tumbling the blocks from one place to another or tossing the smaller ones from one level to the other. If some piece of the setting was not needed for a scene, it was concealed behind the curtains. All of this was done in full view of the audience and to the accompaniment of, and in time with, a spirited march to which the actors had paraded at the beginning of the play. They appeared in single file at one doorway, each actor playing a musical instrument of some kind, paraded around and over the platforms, and disappeared through the opposite doorway as the lights in the auditorium dimmed out. What their music lacked in quality was more than made up for by volume; it was perhaps the most effective method possible to capture the attention of a noisy audience composed of 400 or more children ranging in age from 8 to 13. With the exception of the intermissions there was not a moment when the stage was not filled with action and sound; there was no chance for the young audience to lose interest in what was being presented.

A description of how three of the scenes were handled should suffice to illustrate how effectively and imaginatively the setting was used. The dimming of the house lights on the exit of the last of the parading actors opened the first scene. The curtains above the balcony were opened during the dim-out to reveal Tom and Sid asleep on separate retangular boxes serving as beds (see Plate 72, Fig. 1). Huck moved from darkness into a pool of moonlight near the center of the lower stage and began catcalling to arouse Tom. Tom finally awoke, got out of bed, tiptoed to the window (the U-shaped form on the left side of the balcony), and whispered down to Huck. Tom returned to his bed and dressed, climbed through the window onto the roof, clambered down a tree (the ladder) to the shed roof (small platform), and joined Huck in the yard.

The scene in which Tom, Huck, and Sid decided to become river pirates and set sail on a raft on the Mississippi River was a triumph. Only the bare platforms shown in Fig. 4 were used for this scene. It was treated as a night scene with a single spotlight focused on the small platform down stage. The boys entered the stage through a center opening in the lower curtains their arms filled with pots, pans, blankets, and other camping paraphernalia. This was all carefully loaded and balanced on the supposedly tippy raft (the small platform down front). Tom disappeared through the curtains to return immediately carrying two rubber-tipped poles. Sid took his place on top of the pile of supplies, Tom manned one end of the raft, Huck the other, and they were ready to take off. Lighted by the rays of a single follow spot they shoved the raft (mounted on swivel casters) away from the bank with their rubber-tipped poles and propelled themselves out of the auditorium through one of the big double doors.

Fig. 7 illustrates one of the arrangements used for the interior and exterior scenes of the cave where the Sunday school picnic took place. The curtains above and below the balcony were closed for the exterior scenes, and bright general illumination spread over all the platform area. The children, carrying lunch baskets, entered the brightly lighted area from the doorway stage right. They sang songs, played games, and chased each other around the lower platform levels. The big moment came when a few of them were given lighted candles and they all made ready to enter the cave. The lower curtains were opened slightly at *A* to form the cave entrance, and as the last child disappeared into the cave the general illumination dimmed out. During the dim-out the upper curtains opened and the picnic group reappeared, one at a time, through a trap in the floor just upstage of *B*. The only light on stage was provided by the lighted candles. After exploring the upper level of the cave, the children wrote their initials on the walls with candle smoke and dropped imaginary pebbles from the edge of the balcony into the dark abyss formed by the lower level. Unseen by the rest of the group, Tom and Becky scrambled down the structural forms at *C*, just beneath the balcony stage right, and began to explore the lower level of the cave. They finally disappeared through the curtains at *D* to investigate still another corridor of the cave, and in doing so they became lost. The rest of the children retraced their steps, the upper curtains closed, and the group left the cave's entrance as the lights on the lower levels were again raised. We were once more in the sunshine just outside the entrance of the cave. After the children had gone, variations in the use of levels, curtains, and lights identified the scenes taking place within the cave where Tom and Becky tried to find their way out and where they tried to keep away from Injun Joe who was hiding in the cave. It is hard to conceive of a happier or more imaginative manipulation of scenery for this series of scenes. They would have been difficult, if not impossible, to do had the scenery been designed in a more realistic style.

My Crime

At the Comedy Theatre in Leningrad I saw a delightful production of a French farce called *My Crime*. It told the story of an art student named Madeline who was falsely accused of a crime and placed in prison to await trial. Because she was very beautiful her case attracted much attention, and manufacturers flocked to her side in order to get her endorsement of their products. She was rapidly growing wealthy while still in jail. Eventually the real criminal appeared to claim his just share of the spoils. The very talented director-designer Akimov quite rightly felt that such a theme called for something unusual and amusing in the way of settings. Five stylized settings were used. In four of them an unusual appearance was achieved by use of false perspective; all had restricted acting areas and most unexpected entrance ways.

The play opened with a panoramic view over the roof tops of Paris into Madeline's attic studio (see Plate 73, Fig. 1). Few vertical lines were used for the buildings—everything slanted one way or another; even the balcony surrounding the studio was ramped and slanted toward the stage floor. The only entrance was up a trapped stairway in the hall just outside the studio. A few short scenes took place inside the studio but most of the action was played on the enclosing balcony.

The second scene (Fig. 2) was played in the office of the police commissioner. The walls of the room were formed entirely of black and white filing cabinets, each with prominently identified filing inscriptions. No doors of any kind were visible but it developed that there were entrances in profusion at various unexpected locations. Many unlikely combinations of filing drawers opened up to serve as doorways. The scene was filled with comings and goings, and it seemed that no one used the same doorway twice. There was even a peep hole formed by the filing drawer marked "10" through which the secretary occasionally poked his head.

The third scene, a shallow triangular setting, was Madeline's apartment

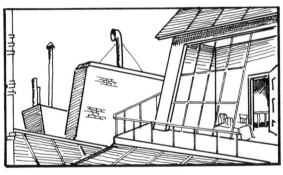

FIG. 1

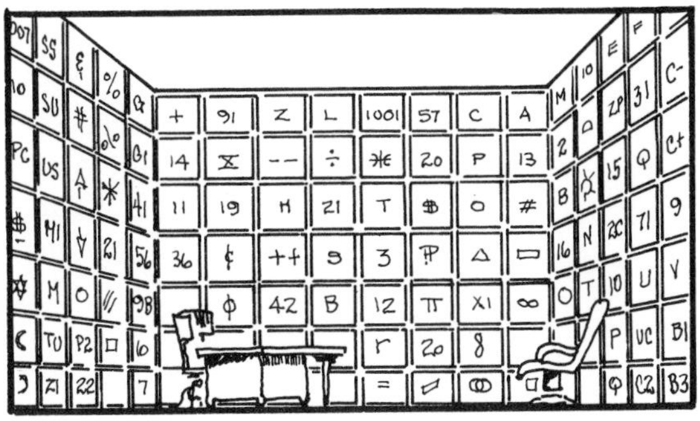

FIG. 2

FIG. 3

FIG. 4

FIG. 5

PLATE 73 *My Crime*, produced at the Comedy Theatre, Leningrad, directed and designed by Akimov

(Fig. 3). The supporting columns and the cornice dipped sharply at the apex of the triangle, giving the room a sense of depth that was belied by the small amount of enclosed floor space. This was crowded with a grand piano and with gifts and flowers for Madeline. The only entrance into the set was from a trap placed upstage of the pile of gifts on stage right.

The designs for the last two scenes, the jury room (Fig. 4) and the lawyer's office (Fig. 5), were drawn by raising the horizon line to an unreasonable level. The settings were then built to correspond exactly to the unnatural view in spite of the restrictions this placed on the acting areas. All of the actors were in place in a seated position when the curtain opened on the jury room. No one entered or left the set, but the sergeant-at-arms did appear momentarily at the practical doorway mounted in the painted drop. Had he attempted to enter the room, he would have fallen some 7′ or 8′ to the stage floor. The jury table was built on a supporting platform raked at an angle of approximately 30°. By the aid of toe straps the foreman of the jury was able to stand when the occasion demanded, but the other jurymen remained seated for obvious reasons.

The lawyer's office was an elaboration of the same general scheme. The only practical acting area was the space enclosed by the ramped, oversized desk, and a narrow platform immediately upstage of it. Entrances to the set were through the doorway cut in the drop. The marquetry floor and the paneled walls were painted on the drop. The columns and the chairs were three-dimensional and attached to the drop in their proper places. The stairway and wall section seen through the doorway were painted on a masking drop.

Akimov had combined an improbable story with improbable settings and imaginative directing to create a production that was completely refreshing and enjoyable.

Intrigue and Love

The production of Schiller's *Intrigue and Love*, by the Vakhtangov Theatre in Moscow, is included here for two reasons. It is another example of the work of Akimov, whom I felt was the most imaginative of the designers whose work I saw in the Soviet Union, and it is an excellent illustration of how simplified designs can be used to solve the complex problems of a play demanding thirteen settings.

The Vakhtangov Theatre was a spacious, well-equipped, comparatively new theatre. This permitted Akimov to employ an elaborate multilevel ramp as a basis for the designs. The ramp, shaped like a large disc, occupied all of the available floor space of the stage. It stood at an angle of about 20° or 25° to the stage floor, an angle that was much too steep to allow an actor to stand or move about on it. The disc was divided into four sections with the divisional lines running parallel to the proscenium opening. The

FIG. 1

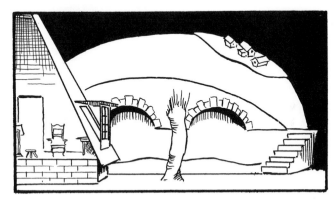

FIG. 2

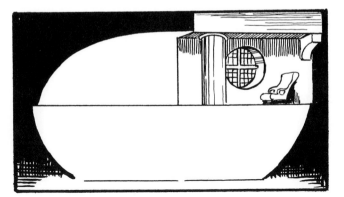

FIG. 3

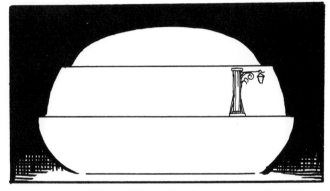

FIG. 4

PLATE 74 *Intrigue and Love*, produced at the Vakhtangov Theatre, Moscow, directed and designed by Akimov

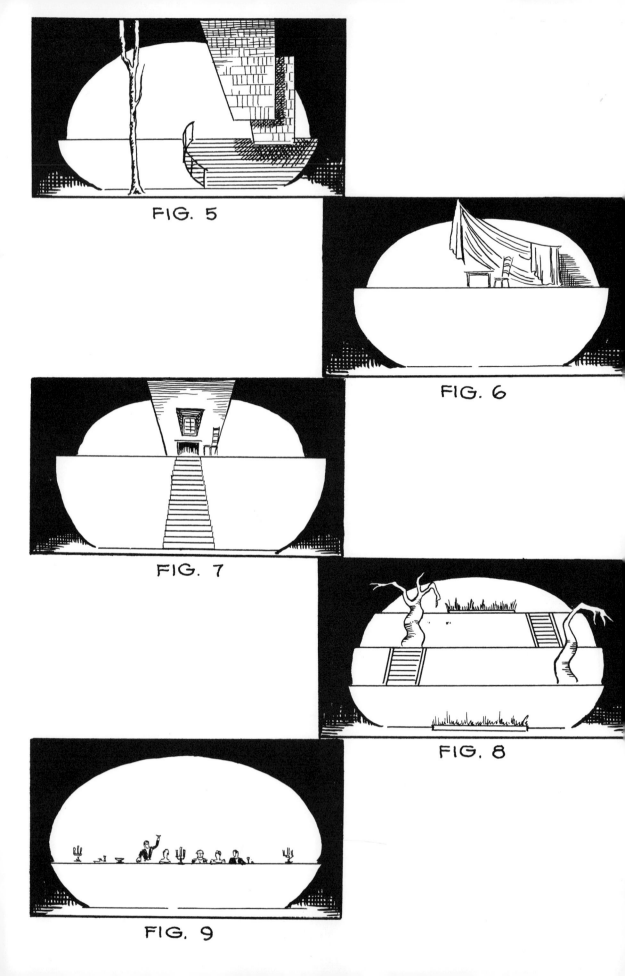

FIG. 5

FIG. 6

FIG. 7

FIG. 8

FIG. 9

FIG. 10

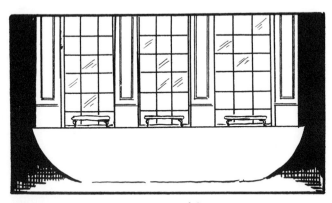

FIG. 11

FIG. 12

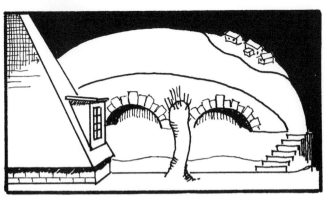

FIG. 13

three upstage sections were mounted on casters and could be moved separately or in combination to expose from one to three perfectly flat acting levels, each at a different height from the stage floor. Black draperies surrounded the disc on three sides and provided masking for the actors as they entered or left any of the three levels. The matted silver surface of the disc resembled a field or terraces covered with snow, a choice of color that was especially appropriate since the action of the play took place in winter.

The interior and exterior of the miller's house (Plate 74, Figs. 2 and 13) were mounted on a wagon which was rolled into position downstage of the disc. All of the rest of the scenery, however, was flown into position on the different acting levels—a scheme of shifting that required very little time.

It is apparent from the sketches how the different settings were used, but two of them deserve special comment. A particularly effective setting was a high wrought-iron gateway and fence that guarded the grounds and buildings of an estate (Fig. 10). The blue-black of the wrought iron was silhouetted against the silver of the disc, and it was not until the gates were opened that one could see a flight of stairs leading upstage to the second acting level.

The setting in Fig. 12 was outstanding for its extreme simplicity of design. It represented a secret rendezvous in the basement of an old house. The two lower acting levels of the disc and the floor space just in front of it were used for this scene. The scene was dimly lighted by a single candle on the table downstage and by a shaft of light, apparently coming from a concealed street light, that cut across the disc at the second acting level. One by one the members of the conclave moved furtively through the shaft of light, down a run of stairs, disappeared through a trap center stage on the first acting level, and reappeared at the doorway of the basement.

Talent and Its Admirers

Those who are handicapped by a lack of stage space may profit by studying the designs and the scheme of shifting used at the Simonov Theatre in Moscow for its production of *Talent and Its Admirers*. The stage of this theatre was extremely small; the proscenium could not have been more than 22′ wide. The proscenium arch was flanked on either side by small doorways facing the audience that gave access to an apron which extended from side wall to side wall of the auditorium.

The play told the story and experiences of a young and attractive actress who was "plagued" by more than her share of suitors. The play moved rapidly from a street scene in front of her home (Plate 75, Fig. 1) to her living room (Fig. 2), a bedroom (Fig. 3), a backstage dressing room (Fig. 4), a box at a theatre (Fig. 5), and finally a beer garden where all of her difficulties were resolved (Fig. 6). The sequence of scenes did not follow the orderly pattern just indicated; it switched from one place to

FIG. 1

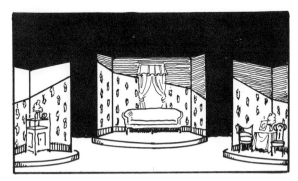

FIG. 2

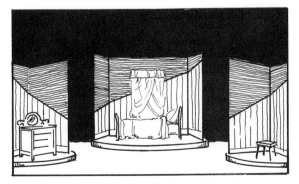

FIG. 3

PLATE 75 *Talent and Its Admirers*, produced at the Simonov Theatre, Moscow

FIG. 4

FIG. 5

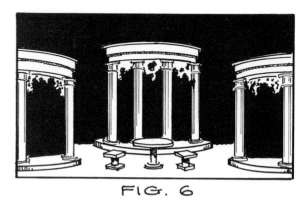

FIG. 6

another and back again so that some of the settings were used several times. It made little difference since the shifts required only seconds to perform and were accomplished in full view of an audience that seemed to enjoy them as much as it did the play.

In the center of the stage was a small revolving unit, perhaps 10′ in diameter. The revolve was divided in half by a supporting frame covered with the same black masking material that enclosed the stage on three sides. What little scenery was used was held in place on the revolve by the supporting frame. On each side of the stage was a smaller revolving unit that extended partially off stage; these were divided into thirds by black supporting frames like the one on the large center revolve. All three of the revolves were used for each scene, each revolve presenting a part of the same scene to the audience. While the scene was being played, the next scene was preset on the center stage and on each of the side stages. At the close of one scene the three revolves were turned simultaneously to bring the following scene into playing position.

Umka

Umka was a modern Russian play concerned with the plight of Siberian natives whose hunting rights were being infringed upon by a group of

FIG. 1

FIG. 2

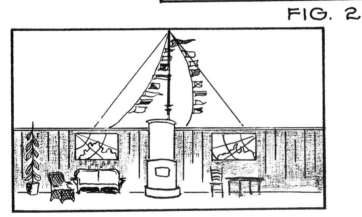

FIG. 3

FIG. 4

PLATE 76 *Umka*, produced at the Theatre of the Revolution, Moscow, designed by Prusskov

FIG. 5

FIG. 6

FIG. 7

FIG. 8

unscrupulous fur traders. A government expedition sets out to right the situation and triggers a series of events that constitute the play.

The Theatre of the Revolution, where this production was presented, was housed in an old theatre that had been a musical and burlesque house, but it had a large comfortable auditorium and a spacious stage that was exceptionally well equipped. In conceiving his designs for the ship, the ice fields, the igloos, and the temporary barracks, designer Prusskov never lost sight of the wealth of stage and lighting equipment that was at his disposal.

In the execution of these designs several of the components of his method of treatment helped to make this production noteworthy. Prusskov used remarkably clear projections of ice fields on an encircling cyclorama to provide a background for his suggestive scenery. Perhaps the most arresting feature of the designs was the substance he chose to simulate a snow covering on the entire stage floor—white fur! The third point, while not directly concerned with scenery, was nevertheless a contributing factor to the success of the production; Prusskov dressed the Siberian characters in authentic native costumes made of fur. All these combined to make the visual impact of the production memorable.

The play opened on an empty stage covered by an expanse of white fur "snow" which was capped by a practical mound of it on center stage. While introductory music was played the encircling cyclorama was filled with projections of constellations, and the audience was then treated to a display of northern lights that gradually displaced the stars. The actors appeared on stage after this scenic introduction (Plate 76, Fig. 1).

The shift from the snow field of the first scene to the second scene aboard a ship (Fig. 2) was made in view of the audience. The mound of snow was revolved until a vertical face of it was toward the audience, thus clearing the downstage area for the ship. The outline of the sailing vessel was two-dimensional, but it was made entirely of strips of white wood. This skeletal ship was lowered into position from the flies. The only practical features of the setting were the cargo cases on the deck and the hand rail adjacent to the proscenium arch. Cloud projections on the cyclorama, formed a very convincing background.

In the third scene (Fig. 3) the signal flags, visible above the top of the temporary barracks wall, were painted on a drop, but they were seen through a gauze placed downstage of the drop. The sound effect of a howling wind combined with the hazy appearance of the signal flags as seen through the gauze gave the impression that the air was filled with driven snow.

Though the constellations and northern lights were tastefully used in the introductory scene, a much more elaborate display in the fourth scene proved a little overwhelming. The dome of snow had been revolved to its first position and supplemented by a practical block of snow placed just upstage of it (Fig. 4). The actors were seen in silhouette against the brilliant sky, and the effect would have been more appropriate in a variety show then in this drama.

Perhaps the most interesting design of the production was the igloo used in the fifth scene (Fig. 5). There was nothing symbolic about it as one might assume from the objects placed above it; the natives habitually suspend their fishing nets between poles to dry, and hang above their igloo the skeleton of a seal as a plea to their gods for good hunting. The igloo, poles, and nets were mounted on a wagon and rolled into place against the vertical face of the snow dome while the skeleton of the seal was lowered into position from the flies. A second igloo interior (Fig. 6) was painted on a drop and placed far downstage to provide a cover scene during one of the heavier scene shifts that took place upstage of it.

The School for Taxpayers

In a crowded room under the first floor of an apartment house was the Zavadski Theatre. Since the floor of the tiny auditorium was perfectly flat the stage floor was raised at the back in the hopes of improving sight lines. Once we had adjusted our chairs to avoid the dripping water pipe overhead, we were treated to a truly delightful evening of theatre-for-fun.

The nonsensical tidbit we saw was a farce entitled *The School for Taxpayers*. It was concerned with the antics of a protagonist who accidentally discovered a scheme whereby he could avoid the payment of taxes and then set up a school to teach others to do the same. Complications with tax collectors were, of course, inevitable, and so the theme developed.

V. A. Zavadski directed the play, and in preliminary discussion with his designer, A. Tischler, Zavadski suggested that the setting should be made as amusing as possible. This Tischler did in a most unusual way. On the tiny stage he built a permanent framework of silver colored pipe which formed a cage; the spaces created by the horizontal and vertical members were each about 2' × 2'6". Sections of the pipe could be removed to form openings that served as windows or doorways. Between the back of the framework and the black draperies that enclosed the set was a sketchily done cutout vaguely resembling the skyline of city buildings.

For the first act the walls of a room were suggested by wicker clothes baskets inserted, bottom side toward the audience, into the openings of the pipe framework (Plate 77, Fig. 1). At about head height and extending around the room was a row of baskets that had been fitted with wall vases, also made of wicker, and each vase was filled with crepe paper flowers. The general effect was not unlike the inside of a giant waffle iron! Even the furniture for all three acts had been especially made of wicker. The chair backs of the first act roughly resembled the torso of a woman holding a wicker flower basket on her head; the uplifted arms of the bleeding tax-

FIG. 1

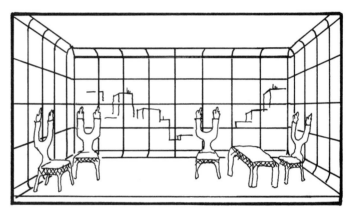

FIG. 2

FIG. 3

PLATE 77   *The School for Taxpayers*, produced at the Zavadski Theatre, Moscow, directed by U. A. Zavadski, designed by A. Tischler

payers were used as chair backs in the second act; while the last act again had chairs with torso backs, but each torso now sported a gay bolero jacket.

The baskets were all removed for the second act and the spaces left open (Fig. 2). In true farcical style the pipe framework was utilized as an oversize jungle gym; the actors were literally all over it!

Baskets were reinserted for the final act, but this time with the bottoms facing off stage (Fig. 3). The audience could now look into each basket, coyly draped with blue plush curtains, to see wall sconces and candles attached in the bottom of alternate baskets.

The Beginning of Life

The Second Moscow Art Theatre produced a new Russian play called *The Beginning of Life*. Its only claim to distinction rested on what Shestakov did with the scenery. The play delineated the dreary life of officers and soldiers of the Red Army assigned to duty somewhere near a battle front. Ruined estates, camp kitchens, officers' billets, battered buildings, and a graveyard suggested the play's locale (Plate 78, Figs. 1-7). I saw the third performance of this play and it may have been still in the throes of revision. However, even the Russian audience seemed impatient with it, and many people left before the play finally ground to a halt.

The Second Moscow Art Theatre was larger and better equipped than many of the theatres I visited. The stage contained a large permanently installed revolve that Shestakov used most effectively. A tremendous ramp, the full width of the large proscenium opening, ran from the upstage limits of the revolving stage past the curtain line and extended far enough into the auditorium to cover the orchestra pit. The slanting face of the ramp had been cut into a circular form directly over the revolving stage. This circular disc was separately braced and supported from the flat floor of the revolve so that it could be turned by it, thus changing the level of the ramp's surface.

It is especially interesting to notice the extreme simplicity of these designs and the manner in which Shestakov repeatedly introduced circular elements of one kind or another into the settings. These curved parts combined nicely with the circular shapes of the exposed segments of the revolve to give the settings a sense of unity that they would not otherwise have possessed.

Life on Wheels

Unlike the theatre district in New York City where most of the theatres are clustered in a relatively small area, the theatres in Moscow were scattered far and wide over the city. This made getting to a theatre something of an adventure, particularly so since the rate of exchange at the time left little money for the luxury of going by taxi. Streetcar trains or electric buses periodically

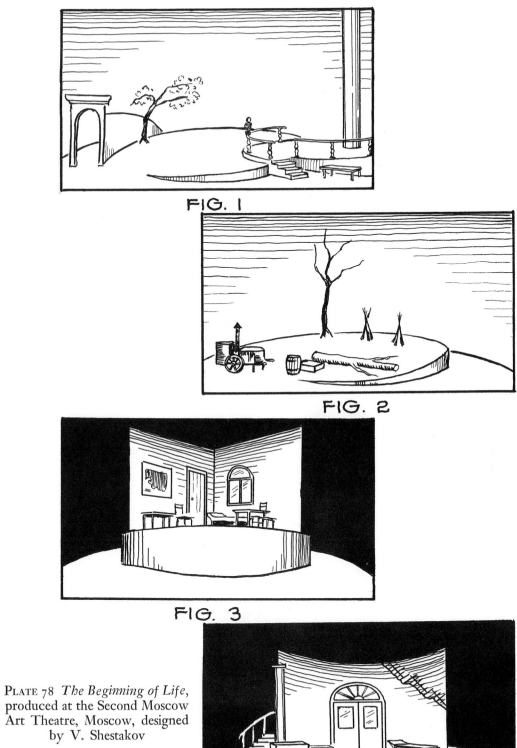

FIG. 1

FIG. 2

FIG. 3

FIG. 4

PLATE 78 *The Beginning of Life*, produced at the Second Moscow Art Theatre, Moscow, designed by V. Shestakov

FIG. 5

FIG. 6

FIG. 7

circled the city, and by taking one of these we could ride to the general vicinity of a theatre, then get off and walk. We usually got lost several times in the process, but we eventually learned to allow time for these side excursions.

We finally located the State Gypsy Theatre in a narrow, unlighted street. A single electric light hung over the entrance which led down a ramp to the basement of a building that had at one time been stately. The area occupied by the theatre had once been an underground restaurant. Tucked into one corner of the room was the smallest stage I had yet seen. The stage floor was raised perhaps 18″ from the auditorium floor and supported a frame proscenium about 20′ wide. The depth of the stage may have been all of 16′ or 18′ while the ceiling limited the grid height to 12′.

The play we were to see was entitled *Life on Wheels,* something akin to a documentary on the life and customs of a band of gypsies. Actually there was little to the play as such, but it did provide an excellent vehicle for a display of the customs, dances, and musical skills of the gypsies who formed

FIG. 1

FIG. 2

FIG. 3

PLATE 79 *Life on Wheels,* produced at the State Gypsy Theatre, Moscow, designed by A. Tischler

FIG. 4

FIG. 5

the acting company. They were an amazing group of talented artists; their zest for life and the spontaneity of their performance was contagious. Everyone in the theatre enjoyed himself as much as the performers.

Tischler, the designer who had created the basket settings for *The School for Taxpayers*, was also responsible for the designs used in this production; and he appeared to excell in overcoming space limitations with ingenious stylized sets. The front curtain of *Life on Wheels* was made of horse collars alternating with gaily colored horse blankets backed by black draperies (Plate 79, Fig. 1). During intermissions the actors reappeared by sticking their heads through the horse collars to perform yet another song.

When the curtain opened on the first act it revealed a dilapidated gypsy wagon backed by a cyclorama made of brilliant colored quilts and horse blankets (Fig. 2). During the following scenes the position of the wagon was shifted to indicate a change of location. We looked into the end of the wagon (Fig. 3) and by splitting it lengthwise and placing the two halves on opposite sides of the stage Tischler contrived to let us see both the inside (Fig. 4) and outside (Fig. 5) of it. A moon was formed for the last scene by sticking a candle in a dishpan and suspending it from the ceiling over the supper dishes below.

BIBLIOGRAPHY

Albright, H. D., W. P. Halstead, and Lee Mitchell, *Principles of Theatre Art*, Boston, Houghton Mifflin, 1955.

Anderson, Donald, *Elements of Design*, New York, Holt, Rinehart and Winston, 1961.

Bieber, Margarete, *History of the Greek and Roman Theatre*, Princeton, N. J., Princeton University Press, 1939.

Brockett, Oscar, *The Theatre, an Introduction*, New York, Holt, Rinehart and Winston, 1964.

Burris-Meyer, Harold, and Edward C. Cole, *Theatres and Auditoriums*, rev. ed., New York, Reinhold, 1966.

Cheney, Sheldon, *Stage Decoration*, New York, John Day, 1928.

Dolman, John, Jr., *The Art of Play Production*, rev. ed., New York, Harper & Row, 1959.

Frederick, Forrest Frank, *Simplified Mechanical Perspective*, Peoria, Ill., Manual Arts Press, 1933.

Freedley, George, and John A. Reeves, *A History of the Theatre*, Crown, 1941.

French, Thomas E., and Carl L. Svensen, *Mechanical Drawing for High Schools*, rev. ed., New York, McGraw-Hill, 1934.

Friederich, Willard J., and John H. Fraser, *Scenery Design for the Amateur Stage*, New York, Macmillan, 1950.

Gillette, A. S., *Stage Scenery, Its Construction and Rigging*, New York, Harper & Row, 1959.

Gruver, Elbert, *The Stage Manager's Handbook*, New York, Harper & Row, 1953.

Guptill, Arthur L., *Color in Sketching and Rendering*, New York, Reinhold, 1935.

Hewitt, Barnard, *Theatre U. S. A. 1668 to 1957*, New York, McGraw-Hill, 1959.

Hewitt, Barnard (ed.), *The Renaissance Stage*, Miami, University of Miami Press, 1958.

Houghton, Norris, *Moscow Rehearsals*, New York, Harcourt, Brace & World, 1936.

Komisarjevsky, Theodore, *Settings and Costumes of the Modern Stage*, New York, Studio Publications, 1933.

Ladd-Franklin, Christine, *Colour and Colour Theories*, New York, Harcourt, Brace & World, 1929.

Lawrenson, T. E., *The French Stage of the XVII Century: A Study in the Advent of the Italian Order*, Manchester, Manchester University Press, 1957.

Luckiesch, Matthew, *Color and Its Applications*, New York, Van Nostrand, 1921.

Macgowan, Kenneth, and William Melnitz, *The Living Stage*, Englewood Cliffs, N. J., Prentice-Hall, 1955.

Meyer, Franz Sales, *Handbook of Ornament*, New York, Dover, 1957.

Nagler, A. M., *Sources of Theatrical History*, New York, Theatre Annual, 1952.

Nicoll, Allardyce, *The Development of the Theatre*, 3rd ed., New York, Harcourt, Brace & World, 1937.

Nicoll, Allardyce, *Masks, Mimes and Miracles*, New York, Harcourt, Brace & World, 1931.

Oenslager, Donald, *Scenery Then and Now*, New York, Norton, 1936.

Oenslager, Donald (ed.), *Notes on Scene Painting by Bradford Ashworth*, New Haven, Conn., Whitlock's, 1952.

Parker, W. Oren, *Sceno-Graphic Techniques*, Pittsburgh, Carnegie Institute of Technology, 1964.

Parker, W. Oren, and Harvey K. Smith, *Scene Design and Stage Lighting*, New York, Holt, Rinehart and Winston, 1963.

Philippi, Herbert, *Stagecraft and Scene Design*, Boston, Houghton Mifflin, 1953.

Sargent, Walter, *Enjoyment and Use of Color*, New York, Scribner, 1923.

Southern, Richard, *Changeable Scenery: Its Origin and Development in the British Theatre*, London, Faber and Faber, 1952.

Southern, Richard, *The Open Stage*, New York, Theatre Arts Books, 1959.

Whiting, Frank M., *The Theatre*, rev. ed., New York, Harper & Row, 1960.

Wright, Edward A., *A Primer for Playgoers*, Englewood Cliffs, N. J., Prentice-Hall, 1958.

INDEX

Abe Lincoln in Illinois, 156
Acting, 3, 8
Adding Machine, The, 174
Akimov, Nikolai, 186
Alice in Wonderland, 163
Analysis of play, 19
Aristophanes, 144

Balance, asymmetrical, 36
    symmetrical, 36
Barefoot in the Park, 34
Basov, 180
Beginning of Life, The, 200, 202
Belasco, David, 148
Benson, Philip, 174
Binder, 124
Blueprinting, 45
Boomerang, 113
Briantzev, A. A., 182
Bridie, James, 21
Brilliance, 37, 40
Brushes, detail, 115–116
    laying-in, 115–116
    priming, 115
    scene paint, 115–116
    transparent water color, 84
Business management, 9
Business manager, 7, 16–17

Capon, William, 146
Carpenter, building, 14
    stage, 14
Caucasian Chalk Circle, The, 171
Center of vision, 62

Chekhov, A., 152
Cheney, Sheldon, 170
Color, 36–37
    elevation, 109
    guide, 91
    qualities of, 37
Coloring the sketch, 89–90
Compass, 47, 119
Composition, elements of, 31, 35–40
Conferences, production staff, 21
Connelly, Marc, 174
Cooperation, production staff, 17
Costume design, relation to scene design,
    4, 7, 9, 16
Country Wife, The, 161
Creativeness, 5
Crew, building, 14
    clean-up, 109
    costume, 16
    light, 15
    sound, 15
    stage, 14
Crucible, The, 157
Cutting plane, 52

Danton's Death, 168
Dark of the Moon, 161
Death of a Salesman, 146
Detail men, 109
Dimensions, encircled, 52
    position of, 53
Directing, 2
Director, 10–12
Distant Drums, 157
Doctor in Spite of Himself, The, 162

Doctor's Dilemma, The, 166
Drafting, instruments, 45–50
　materials, 45
　symbols, 50–51
Draftsman, 13
Drawing, board, 45
　cabinet, 58
　detail, 28
　isometric, 54
　mechanical, 45
　oblique, 56
　sight line, 28, 102–104
Dream Girl, 157
Dream Play, The, 174–175
Duchess of Malfi, The, 177
Dyes, 126

Easiest Way, The, 148
Ekkuklema, 143
Elevations, front, 27, 95, 98–101
　graphed, 109
Emperor Jones, The, 176
Euripides, 36
Exostra, 143
Expressionism, 173–176

Fillers, 109
Form, 36
Formalism, 165–173
French curve, 74

Glue, kinds of, 124–125
　pot, electric, 120
Good Woman of Setzuan, The, 168
Gothic Color Company, 121
Great God Brown, The, 174
Green, Paul, 176
Grigoriev, M. A., 182
Guptill, Arthur, 40
Guthrie, Tyrone, 171

Hairy Ape, The, 174
Hamlet, 164
Harmony, 36
High Tor, 27
Horizon, 62
Howard, Sidney, 23

Hue, 37
　complimentary, 40

Ibsen, Henrik, 152
Illustration board, 84
Importance of Being Earnest, The, 154,
　165
Inge, William, 152
Intrigue and Love, 188–192

Jackson, Brian, 171
Juno and the Paycock, 154

Kaufman, George S., 174
King of the Dark Chamber, The, 168
Komisarjevsky, Theodore, 178

Ladders, 113
Ladd-Franklin, Christine, 40
Layout men, 108
Life on Wheels, 200–204
Lighting, relation to scene design, 7, 9,
　15
Line, 36, 40–41
　center, 51–52
　chalk, 118
　construction, 50–51
　dimension, 51–52
　extension, 51–52
　hidden construction, 51–52
　leader, 51–52
　margin, 50–51
　omission, 51–52
　projection, 51–52
Loutherbourg, Philip, 146
Luckiesch, M., 40

McFarland, Louis, 21
Mass, 36, 40–41
Mechane, 143
Medea, 36
Meyerhold, Vsevelod, 176
Miller, Arthur, 152
Model, designer's, 27
　exhibition, 105
　working, 105
Moiseiwitsch, Tanya, 171
Month in the Country, A, 168

Mrs. McThing, 160
My Crime, 186–188

Naturalism, 150–151

Observation point, 60
Ondine, 162
O'Neill, Eugene, 174, 176
Orthographic projection, 54
Othello, 167, 180–181
Ozlite process, 45

Paint, bins, 114
   boss, 108
   casein, 125
   containers, 116
   crew, organization of, 13, 108
   frame, counterbalanced, 111–112
   frame, stationary, 111
   mixing tables, 113
   scene, 120–123, 125–126
      mixing of, 124
   shop layout, 110
   transparent water colors, 83–85
Palette, rolling scene paint, 116
   transparent water color, 86
Paper, detail, 45
   water color, 84
Paraskenion, 144
Patriots, The, 156
Paul and the Blue Ox, 163
Periaktoi, 143
Perspective, 59
   sketch, 27
Picture plane, 62
Pinakes, 143
Plan, ground, 27–28, 92–94
   horizontal, 105
   master, of stage, 94
Plane, horizontal, 62
   picture, 62
   tormentor, 62
Play, the, 8
   mood of, 31
   spirit of, 31
   technical demands of, 22
Pollux, 143

Production, elements of, 8
   factors common to all, 18
Production staff, 17
Prompter, 12
Properties, 9
   decorative, 33
   selection of, 28–29
Property crew, 15
Property master, 14, 15
Proskenion, 144
Prusskov, 197

Radlov, 180
Realism, 151–154
   pictorial, 154–155
   suggestive, 155–159
Rendering the sketch, 89–90
Research, 26
Rice, Elmer, 157, 174

Saturation, 37
Scale rule, architect's, 48–49
Scene painting, techniques of, 130
   appliqués, 140
   back painting, 140
   base coat, 130
      shaded, 131
   cross hatching, 137
   dipping, 140
   dry brushing, 135–136
   puddling, 138
   rolling, 136–137
   scrumbling, 134
   spattering, 132–133
      masked, 133
   stenciling, 138–139
   stippling, 135
Scene shop, 25
Scenery, portability of, 43
Schiller, Friedrich von, 188
School for Taxpayers, The, 163, 198–
   200, 204
Second Moscow Art Theatre, 23
Sequence, 36
Section, horizontal, 105
   vertical, 105
Sectional shading, 52
Setting, drapery, 165–166

Setting (*Continued*)
  trimming and decorating of, 29
  unit, 168–169
Shade, 40
Shakespeare, William, 180
Shestakov, V., 200
Sight lines, 24–25, 94, 102
Simon, Neil, 34
Simonov Theatre, 23, 192–193
Sizing, 129
Sizing water, 125
Sketch, designer's, 26
  thumbnail, 79
  water color, 82
Specifications, 44
Spray gun, 119
Stage, architectural, 170–173
  arena, 166–167
  master plan of, 94
Stage equipment, 24
Stage lighting, 3
Stage manager, 12
Stevens, T. W., 21
Straight edge, 117–118
Stravinsky, Igor, 176
Streetcar Named Desire, A, 146
Stylization, 159–163

Tairov, Alexander, 176
Tale of a Soldier, The, 176

Talent and Its Admirers, 192–193
Technical production, 3
Technician, 7, 13
Theatre, functional, 144
Thorp, Thaddeus, 174
Tint, 40
Tischler, A., 163
Tobias and the Angel, 21
Tom Sawyer, 182–186
Tone, 40
Tormentors, 65
Traviata, La, 156
Tread the Green Grass, 176
Trespassers, 168
Triangles, 46–47
T square, 46
Twelfth Night, 23

Umka, 194–196

Vanishing point, 65
  central, 70

Williams, Tennessee, 152
Windsor and Newton, Ltd., 85

Yellow Jack, 23

Zavadski, V. A., 198
Zola, Emile, 150